Rembrandt
By Josef Israels

Turner
By C. Lewis Hind

Turner
By W. Cosmo Monkhouse

The Art of Katsuhiro Otomo
By Jeremy Robinson

The Art of Masamune Shirow
By Jeremy Robinson

ARTBOOKS

FROM CRESCENT MOON
PUBLISHING

Leonardo da Vinci
by James Pearson

Early Netherlandish Painting
by Rosalind Mutter

Memling
By W.H.J. & J.C. Weale

Van Eyck
By J. Cyril M. Weale

Piero della Francesca
by Naomi Haskell

Giovanni Bellini
by Julia Davis

Eric Gill: Nuptials of God
by Anthony Hoyland

*Minimal Art and Artists In the
1960s and After*
by Laura Garrard

*Vincent van Gogh: Visionary
Landscapes*
by Stuart Morris

*Mark Rothko: The Art of
Transcendence*
by Julia Davis

Jasper Johns
by L.M. Poole

Brice Marden
by Laura Garrard

*Frank Stella: American Abstract
Artist*
by James Pearson

*Maurice Sendak and the Art of
Children's Book Illustration*
by L.M. Poole

*Sex in Art: Pornography and
Pleasure in Painting and
Sculpture*
by Cassidy Hughes

The Art of Andy Goldsworthy
by William Malpas

*Andy Goldsworthy: Touching
Nature*
by William Malpas

Andy Goldsworthy In Close-Up
by William Malpas

Andy Goldsworthy In America
by William Malpas

Andy Goldsworthy: Pocket Guide
by William Malpas

The Art of Richard Long
by William Malpas

Richard Long: Pocket Guide
by William Malpas

*Constantin Brancusi: Sculpting the
Essence of Things*
by James Pearson

*Alison Wilding: The Embrace of
Sculpture*
by Susan Quinnell

Erotic Art In the 19th Century
By Cassidy Hughes

Erotic Art In the Renaissance
By Cassidy Hughes

Erotic Art
By Cassidy Hughes

The Erotic Object: Sexuality in
Sculpture From Prehistory to the
Present Day
by Susan Quinnell

Land Art: A Complete Guide
by William Malpas

Land Art In Close-Up
by William Malpas

Land Art In Great Britain
by William Malpas

Land Art In the U.S.A.
by William Malpas

Installation Art In Close-Up
by William Malpas

Colorfield Painting
by Laura Garrard

Bellini
By James Mason

Botticelli
By Henry Binns

Renaissance In Italy: The Fine
Arts
By John Addington Symonds

The Life of Michelangelo
Buonarroti
By John Addington Symonds

Michelangelo Buonarroti
By Charles Holroyd

Michelangelo
By Estelle Hurll

Michelangelo
By Romain Rolland

Correggio
By Estelle M. Hurll

Tintoretto
By S.L. Bensusan

Titian: A Collection of Fifteen
Pictures
By Estelle M. Hurll

The Earlier Work of Titian
By Claude Phillips

The Later Work of Titian
By Claude Phillips

The Earlier and Later Work of
Titian
By Claude Phillips

Bernardino Luini
By James Mason

Perugino
By Selwyn Brinton

Perugino
By George Williamson

Raphael
By Estelle M. Hurll

Raphael
By Paul Konody

Dante Gabriel Rossetti
By Esther Wood

Recollections of Dante Gabriel
Rossetti
By T. Hall Caine

Burne-Jones
By A. Lys Baldry

The Whistler Book
By Sadakichi Hartmann

INGRES

INGRES

MASTERS IN ART

CRESCENT MOON

First published 1906. This edition © 2021. Reprint 2024.

Set in Book Antiqua 10 on 14pt.
Designed by Radiance Graphics.

Thanks to the authors and publishers quoted.

British Library Cataloguing in Publication data

ISBN-13 9781861718051
ISBN-13 9781861719065

CRESCENT MOON PUBLISHING
P.O. Box 1312, Maidstone, Kent, ME14 5XU
Great Britain, www.crmoon.com

CONTENTS

NOTE ON THE TEXT

The text is from *Ingres*, in the *Masters In Art* series, part 79, volume 7, published by Bates and Guild Company, Boston, 1906.

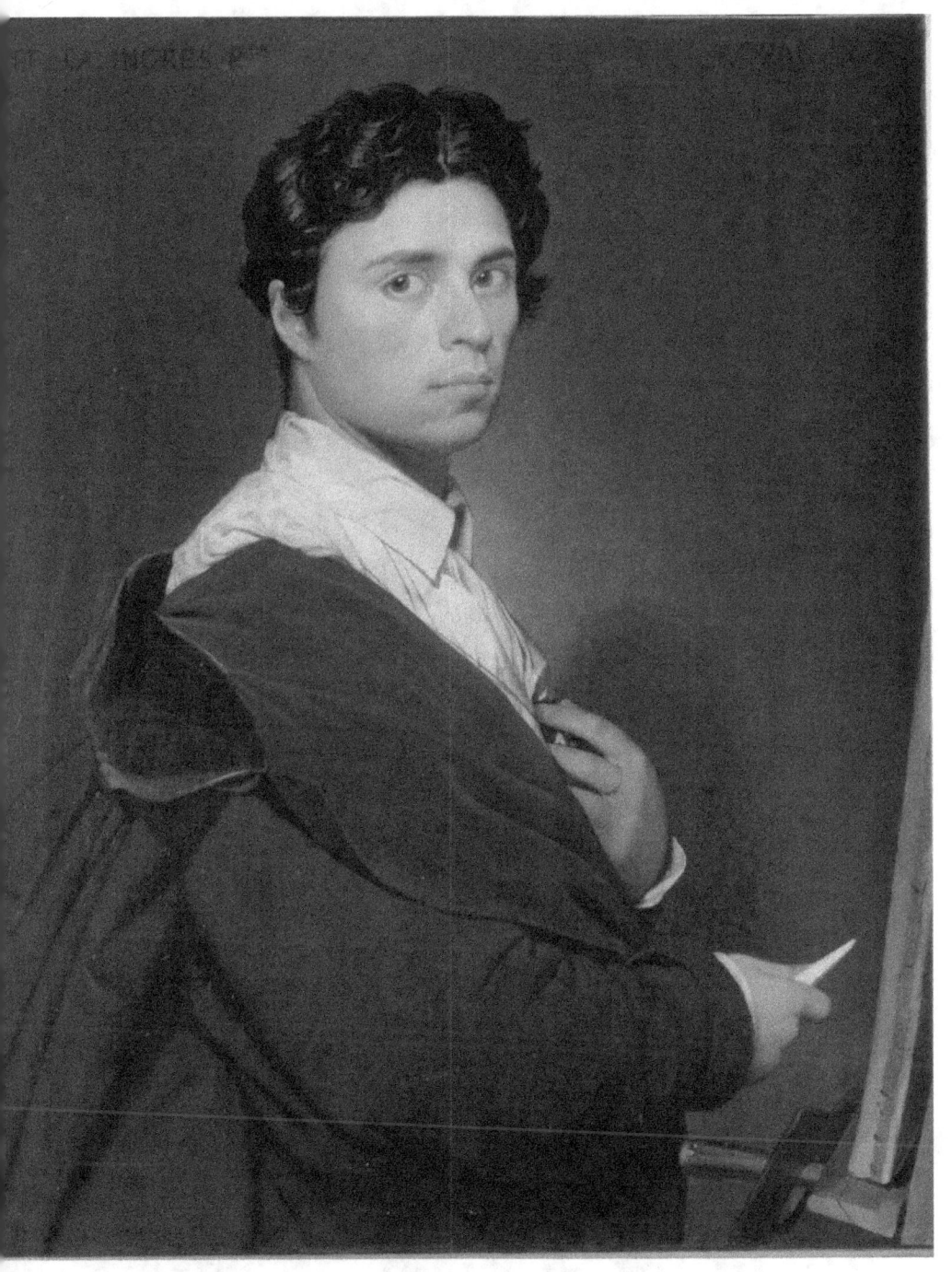

J.A.D. Ingres, Self-Portrait, 1804, Louvre

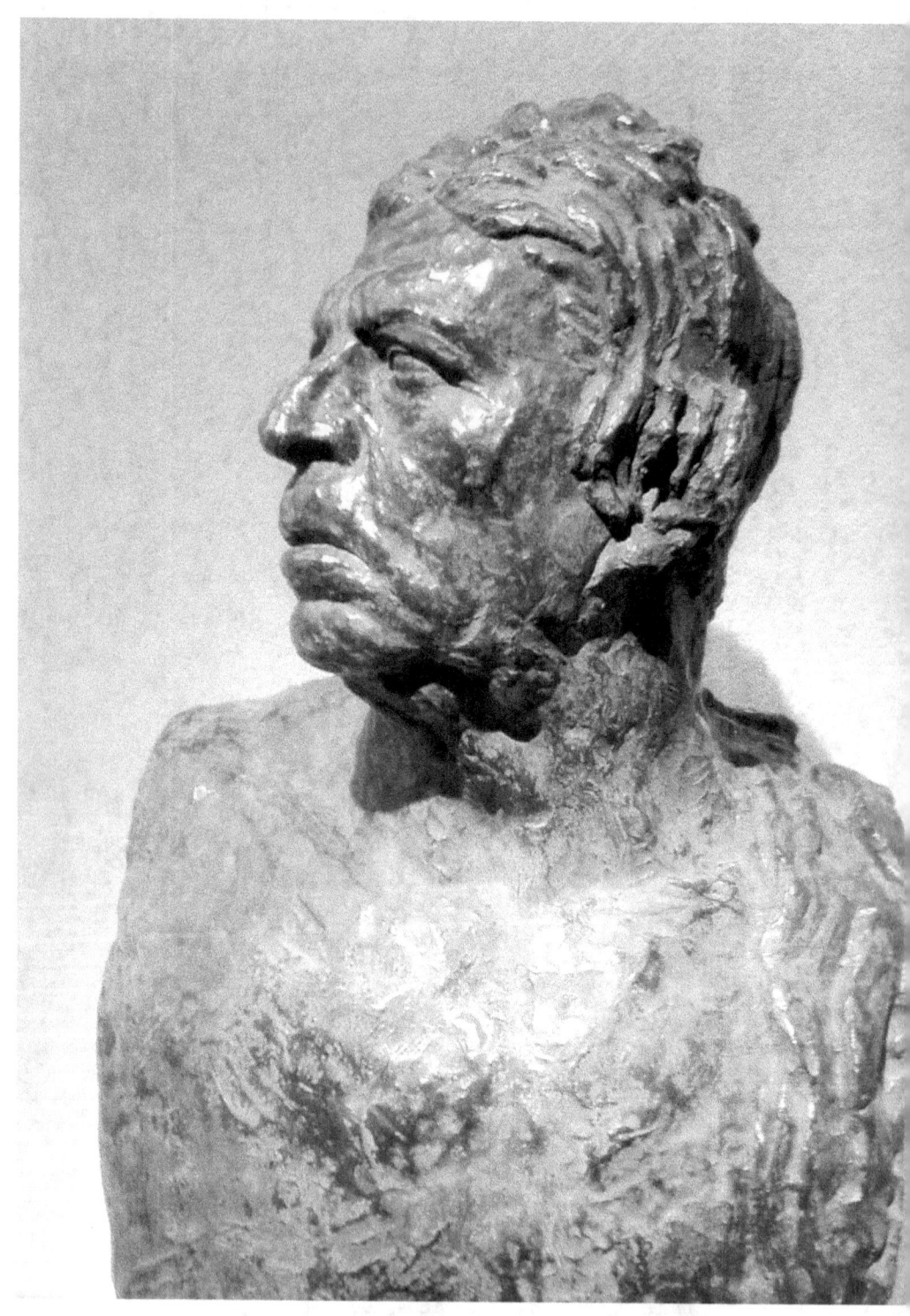

Antoine Bourdelle, Ingres, Musée Antoine Bourdelle

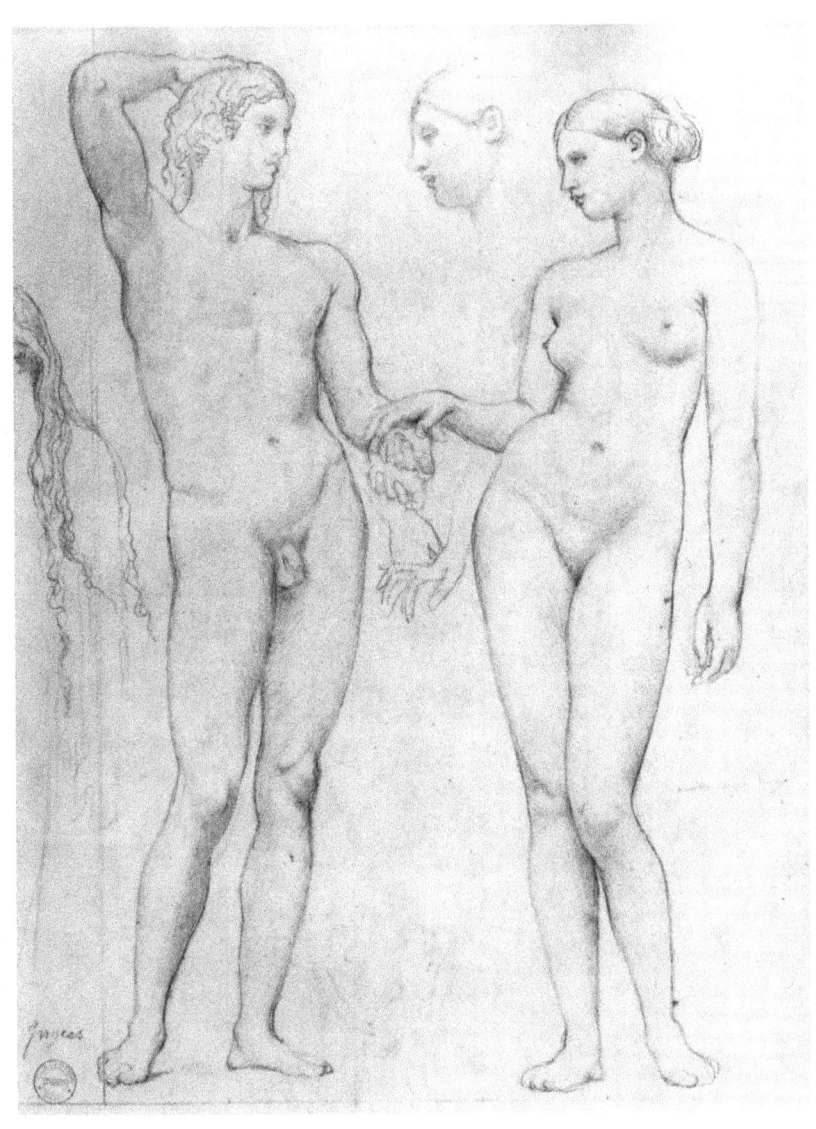

J.A.D. Ingres, Study For L'Age d'Or, 1862

The Life of
Jean-Auguste-Dominique Ingres

BORN 1780: DIED 1867
FRENCH SCHOOL

Jean-Auguste-Dominique Ingres (pronounced Ang´gr) was born at Montauban in the south of France, on August 29, 1780. His father, Jean-Marie-Joseph Ingres, was by profession a house-decorator, with talents so versatile that he was also to some extent painter, sculptor, architect, and musician as well. It was he who gave the first instruction in drawing and in music to his son, who, from the outset, showed so much ability in both that it was a question which should be adopted as his life-work.

Apparently the boy received but little schooling, but before he was twelve years old had acquired such proficiency as a violinist that he was accepted as a member of the orchestra of the theater of Toulouse, where on one memorable occasion he played a concerto by Viotti so skilfully that it called forth hearty applause. Deeming music to be more remunerative than painting, his parents wished him to devote himself to it professionally. This did not, however, prevent their sending him to the painter Vigan, in Toulouse, for instruction in drawing, and under his guidance Ingres followed the course prescribed by the Academy of that city, in which Vigan was a professor. Later he entered the studio of Roques, a painter who had been associated in Rome with Vien and David, but who, while adhering to their doctrines, had devoted much time to copying the works of the great Italians of the Renaissance. The sight of these copies – above all, of one of Raphael's 'Madonna of the Chair' – revealed to Ingres his true vocation, and thenceforth no doubt existed in his mind that he would devote his life to art.

Whatever disappointment his parents may have felt to have the matter so decided, no opposition was made to his determination, and after a brief period of study under a landscape-painter – Briant, or, as M. Momméja says, Bertrand, by name – he started for Paris. There he soon obtained admission to the studio of Jacques-Louis David, then the acknowledged leader of the school of painting in France.

This was in 1796, and for the next four years Ingres worked diligently and with such effect that before long he was recognized as one of David's most promising pupils. A proof of his master's appreciation of his ability is the fact that when called upon to paint a portrait of Madame Récamier (see Masters in Art, Part 74, Vol. 7) David selected his young pupil Ingres to assist him in the work. But harmony between master and pupil was of short duration, and although to the end of his life Ingres spoke with admiration of "the great David and his great school," asserting that his teaching was established "on the severest and the truest principles," friction arose between them, so that in the competition for the grand prize of Rome in 1800, Ingres, unjustly it was said, was awarded but the second prize. In the following year David's jealousy was aroused by the praise bestowed by the English sculptor Flaxman upon the composition by Ingres of 'Achilles and the Ambassadors of Agamemnon,' which won for its author the grand prize of Rome.

At length, in 1806, he was enabled to go to Italy, where he remained for eighteen years, during the first five of which he was a pensioner of the French Academy in Rome, then established in the Villa Medici. He now found himself able to study at the fountainhead both ancient and Renaissance art, and was

Although the young painter was now entitled to a sojourn of five years in Italy, such was the reduced state of the French national finances that his departure for Rome was indefinitely postponed. In the meantime he was accorded a studio in the deserted convent of the Capuchins in Paris, where with several other artists he pursued his studies. Poor and without commissions, save a few chance orders, or a stray job for some bookseller, Ingres worked assiduously at drawings and studies in color, producing also a number of works which have since become famous – a portrait of his father, one of himself at twenty-four (now at Chantilly), portraits of Monsieur and Madame Rivière (in the Louvre), 'La belle Zélie' (Rouen Museum), two portraits of Napoleon Bonaparte, and others, in which, as Delaborde has said, "he showed, as boldly and forcibly as at the end of his career, all the strong, realistic qualities which form the basis of his art."

At length, in 1806, he was enabled to go to Italy, where he remained for eighteen years, during the first five of which he was a pensioner of the French Academy in Rome, then established in the Villa Medici. He now found himself able to study at the fountainhead both ancient and Renaissance art, and was transported by the beauty of the works of the sixteenth-century Italian painters – especially by those of Raphael, whom he always regarded as the greatest of all masters.

Ingres' work gained steadily in strength and vigor, and his individuality developed rapidly. Departing from the cold formalism of David, he turned to nature for his inspiration and gave a greater semblance of life to his figures than was in strict accordance with the code of the classicists. 'Œdipus and the Sphinx,' the first work sent by him from Rome to Paris, gave evidence that the young pensioner of the French Academy was already in possession of his powers, and that however severely he might be criticized for the singularity of his works, he was undoubtedly some one to be counted with.

Soon after painting his 'Œdipus' he began the 'Venus Anadyomene' which was finished many years later. These works were followed by some of his finest portraits, and, in 1811, he completed 'Jupiter and Thetis,' a large canvas now in the Museum of Aix. 'Romulus and Acron' and 'Virgil reading the Æneid' followed; then came 'The Betrothal of Raphael,' 'Don Pedro kissing the Sword of Henry iv.', 'The Sistine Chapel,' and 'The Large Odalisque.' 'The Death of Leonardo da Vinci' and 'Henry iv. and the Spanish Ambassador' were painted in 1817; 'Roger liberating Angelica' and 'Francesca da Rimini' were finished two years later. But whatever the subject or the treatment, none of his works found favor in France. The classicists looked upon him as a renegade from their ranks, and, strangely enough, it was only by Delacroix and a few others of the so-called romanticists (regarded by Ingres with openly expressed abhorrence) that the merit of his works seems at that time to have been recognized.

As year after year passed by, and neither reputation nor money rewarded his efforts, the cold indifference and neglect of his country were keenly felt by him. He was, however, so firmly convinced that his methods were the true ones – that for an attainment of the highest style an artist must turn to nature, and that color and effect should be wholly subordinate to beauty of line – that, even when sore pressed and in the utmost need, he never deviated from his path in order to cater to popular prejudice and prevailing taste. "I count on my old age to avenge me," he used to say.

In 1813, when he was thirty-three, Ingres married a young French woman, Madeleine Chapelle by name, who, in a rather business-like way, had gone to Rome from her home in Montauban at the invitation of some relatives living in Italy with whom Ingres had become well acquainted, for the express purpose of becoming the artist's wife. The marriage was a congenial and perfectly happy one. Madame Ingres seems from the first to have felt firm faith in her husband's genius, and he owed much to her unfailing courage and devotion. The burden of his poverty was cheerfully assumed by her; all petty annoyances, as well as serious anxieties, were kept from his knowledge so far as was possible, and with no thought but of his well-being and his peace of mind, his wife shared his trials and lightened his cares.

It was at this period that Ingres, in order to earn money enough for their daily bread, executed for slight remuneration many of those marvelous little portraits in lead-pencil (see plates iii, iv, and v) which are so exquisite in touch, so perfect in their purity of line, that they place him on a level with the most consummate draftsmen of all times. He himself seems to have regarded these little masterpieces, for they are nothing less, merely as "pot-boilers," and to have even experienced a certain sense of humiliation that his art should perforce be turned into a channel so trivial in his eyes compared with the great works his brush longed to paint. The story is told of a gentleman who one day knocked at the door of his modest studio in Rome, and when Ingres himself appeared, asked timidly, "Does the artist live here who draws portraits in lead-pencil?" "No, sir," was the angry reply; "he who lives here is a painter," and the door was slammed in the face of the astonished visitor. Yet that he did appreciate their artistic excellence is clear from the fact that when in 1855 it was proposed to hang a row of these drawings below the paintings in his exhibition of that year, he objected. "No," he said, "people would look only at them."

In 1820, after painting for one of the churches in Rome a large picture representing 'Christ giving the Keys to St. Peter' (now in the Louvre), Ingres left Rome, and, in the hope of better fortune than had so far attended him in Italy, settled in Florence. His friend and former fellow-pupil in David's studio, the sculptor Bartolini, was then living there, and did all in his power to assist him; but Bartolini's kindness served to only alleviate, not to overcome, the hardships of this residence in a city where Ingres was all but unknown, and where he was without even the scanty means of support afforded by the sale of his pencil portraits, which in Rome had been in demand by the strangers constantly passing through that city. He and his wife were indeed so poor that often they had not money enough to buy the necessary food. And yet at the time of their greatest distress he bravely rejected the proposition of a wealthy Englishman to go to England, where a fortune would be assured him by the execution of portraits in lead-pencil.

The work that chiefly occupied the artist in Florence was completing a picture entitled 'The Entry of Charles v. into Paris,' and in filling an order received from the French Administration of the Fine Arts for a large picture for the Cathedral of Montauban, representing 'The Vow of Louis xiii.' When at work upon this painting he received a visit one day from Delécluze, another fellow-pupil in the David studio, who, passing through Florence, had hunted up his old friend. Delécluze was struck by the imposing character of the picture, and urged the artist, who was discouraged and disheartened and talked of abandoning the work altogether, to complete it and send it to Paris. This was done, and when, a year later, 'The Vow of Louis xiii.' was exhibited at the famous Salon of 1824 Ingres had the gratification of knowing that at last recognition had come to him. The picture met with universal approbation, and Ingres, who now returned to France after a self-imposed exile of eighteen years, became suddenly famous. At Montauban he was received with enthusiasm; in Paris he was decorated with the badge of the Legion of Honor, and in the following year, 1825, was elected to the Institute of France.

The French government now commissioned him to execute a ceiling decoration for one of the galleries of the Louvre. The result was 'The Apotheosis of Homer,' the greatest of all his subject-pictures. This was in 1827, and from then on Ingres was looked upon as a leader of the French school – a *chef d'école*. His studio was thronged with pupils as David's once had been – the two Flandrins, Amaury-Duval, Chassériau, Lehmann, Pichon, and the brothers Balze were among the number – and with authority only less despotic than that of his former master, he ruled the band of young artists who regarded him with such admiration and reverence that they brooked no adverse criticism of him whom they felt to be the deliverer from the bondage of the severe classicism of David, and, at the same time, the opponent of that romantic reaction which was daily growing in power under the leadership of Eugène Delacroix.

Ingres himself was vehement in his denunciation of this new movement, which, diametrically opposed to the academic and the classic, rated freedom of expression and the representation of dramatic and emotional themes as superior to formal composition and impersonal, statuesque art, and held that beauty of color was of greater pictorial importance than purity of line. His animosity to Delacroix, then the leader of the romanticists, knew no bounds. He regarded him as a follower of the evil one, and could not hear his name mentioned with equanimity. Ingres was violent and prejudiced by nature, and holding as he did that "drawing was the probity of art," and that painting was but a development of sculpture, he felt that the kind of art practised by Delacroix and his school was nothing short of blasphemous. This feeling of hostility was fully reciprocated by the romanticists. Party feeling ran high and was increased by the intense partisanship shown to their leaders by the students and younger painters belonging to the opposing factions.

In 1834 Ingres' great canvas 'The Martyrdom of St. Symphorien' was exhibited at the Salon. The reception accorded it was far from what its author, who regarded it as one of his finest achievements, had counted on. Filled with anger and resentment that the same cold indifference that had greeted his early efforts was shown this picture, Ingres, in disgust, resolved to work no more for the unappreciative public, and gladly accepted the offer of the directorship of the French Academy in Rome.

During his second sojourn in Italy he produced but few works. 'The Virgin of the Host,' a portrait of Cherubini, a small version of the 'Odalisque,' and a picture of 'Stratonice' are the principal pictures of this period. His duties as Director of the Academy were conscientiously fulfilled, and in the congenial atmosphere of Rome, surrounded by his pupils, seven years passed.

In 1841, his picture of 'Stratonice,' painted for the Duke of Orleans, and now at Chantilly, was sent from Rome to Paris and exhibited at the Palais Royal. The reception it met with was highly favorable, and decided its author to return once more to his own country. Arrived in Paris, Ingres was received with all due deference; a banquet was given in his honor, at which painters, sculptors, and musicians united in showing him their admiration and respect. Delacroix alone was conspicuous by his absence.

A portrait of the Duke of Orleans was one of the first works executed by Ingres after his return, and before long he received the flattering commission from the Duke of Luynes to decorate with two great mural paintings the large hall of that nobleman's château at Dampierre. For many years this work continued, Ingres and his wife spending several weeks each spring as guests of the Duke of Luynes in order that the painter might pursue his labors under the most favorable conditions. The subjects to be portrayed were 'The Iron Age' and 'The Golden Age,' but an unfortunate combination of circumstances prevented the completion of either one. At first Ingres worked with enthusiasm, but as time went on his ardor cooled. Misunderstandings arose between the duke and the painter, and when, in 1849, the wife, who for nearly forty years had been his faithful and devoted companion, died, Ingres lost all heart to go on with the task, and the contract with the Duke of Luynes was canceled.

His wife's death left him desolate. He worked as diligently as ever, but his loneliness preyed upon him, and, embittered as he was by the struggles and privations of his early life, he could ill bear the loss of one on whom he had learned to depend for comfort and counsel. His friends all urged him to marry again, and accordingly, in 1852, he married Mademoiselle Delphine Ramel, some thirty years younger than he and the niece of one of his closest friends, and found in her a devoted companion who cheered his closing years.

In 1853 his most important work was 'The Apotheosis of Napoleon I.,' painted for the ceiling of a hall in the Hôtel de Ville, Paris, a work that was destroyed by the communards in 1871.

At the Universal Exposition held in Paris in 1855, the master, then seventy-five years of age, consented to exhibit a collection of his works. A room was reserved for them exclusively, and the impression they produced was such that Prince Napoleon, president of the jury, proposed an exceptional reward for the painter, who was named by the emperor Grand Officer of the Legion of Honor.

In the following year Ingres completed one of his most beautiful and most famous works, known as 'La Source.' Begun many years before, this picture is the culmination, so to speak, of his genius, the crowning-point of his task, his final word. After years of disappointed hopes, of struggle and of neglect, the artist now in his old age rested secure in the glory which was his at last.

After the completion of 'La Source' Ingres occupied himself chiefly in finishing many of the studies made in his younger days, and in painting replicas of several of his pictures. In 1862, when over eighty, he completed a large canvas, commissioned many years before by Queen Marie Amélie, wife of Louis

Philippe. This work, representing 'Christ among the Doctors,' is now in the Museum of Montauban, to which the artist bequeathed it at his death, together with his painting of 'Ossian's Dream,' a collection of his drawings and studies, as well as marbles, bronzes, medals, vases, pictures, books and engravings, his favorite pieces of furniture, his easel, palette, brushes, and his famous violin on which almost to the last he played with unusual skill.

In the same year that saw the completion of his 'Jesus among the Doctors' an exposition was held in his honor at Montauban, when Ingres, who was present on the occasion, was greeted with an ovation by his fellow-townsmen, who presented him with a crown of gold. Not long afterwards he received news of his appointment as a senator of France – a flattering testimony to his genius and the highest dignity which had ever been accorded an artist in that country.

Ingres' last years passed peacefully. His great delight was in his work and in music. Early in January, 1867, he became absorbed in a plan of hearing in his own home before he died some of the music of the composers he most deeply cared for – Gluck, Haydn, Beethoven, and Mozart. A chamber concert was accordingly arranged, and a number of his special friends were invited to the festival, which opened with a grand dinner. Ingres – "Father Ingres," as he was called – was in the best of spirits, and, notwithstanding his advanced age, seemingly in the best of health. Although too old to himself play on his violin, he had lost none of his keen enjoyment of music, and on this occasion his enthusiasm was that of youth. He listened enraptured to the works of his favorite composers played by some of the most skilled musicians of Paris, and finally begged that before the evening was over he might hear the concerto by Viotti which, as a boy of twelve, he had played in the theater at Toulouse.

During the night following this memorable little concert Ingres was awakened by the fall of a burning log from the fireplace to the floor of his chamber. Instead of ringing for a servant, he himself restored the log to its place and opened the window to free the room from smoke. In the few moments this occupied he took a severe cold. A cough developed, and one week later, on January 14, 1867, he died, in the eighty-seventh year of his age.

His funeral was held three days afterwards. An immense crowd followed the hearse which conveyed his remains from his home on the Quai Voltaire, Paris, to the Church of St. Thomas Aquinas, where the services were held, and thence to the cemetery of Père-Lachaise, where he was laid to rest.

In addition to the honors which had been conferred upon Ingres by his own country, he had been elected a member of the Academies of Florence, Amsterdam, Antwerp, Berlin, and Vienna; had been made a Chevalier of the Order of Civil Merit of Prussia; a Commander of the Order of Leopold of Belgium; a Chevalier of the Order of St. Joseph of Tuscany; and had received the grand cross of the Order of Guadaloupe.

THE ART OF INGRES

CHARLES BLANC
'GAZETTE DES BEAUX-ARTS', 1868

We have heard eminent artists, who in other respects admired Ingres, deplore the influence he exercised upon the French school of painting by reason of the despotic nature of his teaching and the fact that his eccentric sayings, regarded as they were as oracular, unfortunately carried with them in the eyes of his prejudiced followers all the weight of serious opinions. Such criticism has given us food for thought, and it is not without having duly considered it that we now express our views regarding Ingres and the rôle he played as leader of the French school....

The violent reaction of the romanticists against the too-sculptural tendencies of David led, as all reactions do lead, to another extreme. Arriving in France, as he did after his sojourn in Italy, in the midst of the fray, Ingres saw with astonishing clearness in what respects the school of David had erred, and also what justice there was at bottom in the revolt of the romanticists. He saw that in a generalization of form, in an adoption of the type of statues, of the Greek profile, and of sculpturesque draperies, a cold and conventional quality had been imparted to the painting of his former co-disciples. Struck by what was natural, interesting, and essentially naïve in the work of the Italian artists of the fifteenth century, he felt that true style was only to be obtained from a profound study of nature, which alone produces an endless variety of forms; that any general type of beauty must be modified by a reference to the individual – if need be, even by characteristic ugliness – and that, finally, universal truth could be attained only by a treatment of individual truth. In this he was more of a painter than David; he reformed the reform of his master.

Ingres, then, was the first to have a conception of actual truth; the first to know that in art the ideal is the quintessence of the real; that style should be derived not from erudition, but from life; that it may be acquired from the most commonplace models; that it must be *human*....

In leading the French school back to a study of nature, he purged it from two evils, called in the language of the studios *chic* and *poncif*. The first signifies the fashion of painting from memory, from practice, without consulting nature. The second signifies the habit of repeating forms learned by heart. From these two banes of art Ingres delivered painting in France, thereby rendering it an inestimable service. While giving satisfaction to the romanticists in recognizing that their reaction was to some extent justifiable, he perceived at the same time, and just as clearly, that romanticism was a return to the decadence. Indeed, since it had burst into being, only those painters were admired who, essentially imitators, were called in Italy *naturalisti*. Caravaggio, Ribera, Guercino, Zurbaran, Manfredi, Solimena – all were lauded. Nothing was talked of but "solid painting," "solidity of technique," "painting with a full brush." The sublime beauties of fresco were forgotten, as were the men who had found expression in the grand, the universal art of design. It seemed, forsooth, as if art had begun in the seventeenth century, for in the estimation of these innovators the first of all masters, after Veronese, was Rubens, and according to them Rubens had but one equal – Rembrandt. What they admired in Rembrandt, however, was not exactly his genius, his poetic invention, and the delicacy of his marvelously expressive drawing; but the freedom, the boldness, of his style, the so-called secrets of his etchings, the intensity of his famous lights, contrasting with the transparency of his underpainting – all the alchemy of his mysterious methods.

From these departures from the established methods of the French school Ingres in his turn reacted, and as he was convinced that he was right and was by nature violent, he reacted with conviction and with violence. He loved nature but not naturalism. He was willing that his pupils should salute Rubens, but they must not pause before him in the Louvre, but pass on to Perugino, Raphael, Leonardo da Vinci, Fra Bartolommeo, Andrea del Sarto. All beautiful variations of color were to his mind inferior to the eloquence of form. The affectation of searching for effect seemed to him a means of degrading painting to the level of the theatrical. To the decorators of Venice he preferred the draftsmen of Florence; to Delacroix, he preferred Ingres.

Thus the painter of 'The Vow of Louis xiii.' and of 'St. Symphorien' stood half way between the cold idealism of the classicists and the brutal realism of the romanticists. It is but just to say, however, that in his *teaching* Ingres was wholly one-sided, thinking no doubt that to gain a little, much must be demanded. In teaching that "drawing is everything, that all may be expressed by line, even smoke," he tended towards painting without relief, devoid of all planes. By dint of preaching austerity of tone and training his pupils to beware of colorists, he veiled his whole school in gray. The logical outcome of this was to drive painting into an extreme directly opposed to that which he wished to avoid; that is to say, into the dryness of sharply defined contours and a contempt for methods purely picturesque.

Such was unquestionably the harmful side of Ingres' influence. But, on the other hand, it was he who taught, by his works even more than by his words, that nature is idealized by freeing her from all unimportant details, by selecting only her significant traits; that in order not to petrify forms by generalizing them, we must simplify types by individual characteristics taken directly from life; that drawing, which appeals to the heart, is superior to color, which pleases the eye; that nude figures are more beautiful than clothed; that drapery is more artistic than costume; that the portrayal of human passions, in that they are eternal, is superior to any ethnographical representation of changing manners. In a word, that there is a higher and a lower order of art....

So powerful was the influence of this great artist as leader of the French school that it extended to all branches of art. Painting, sculpture, engraving, even architecture and music, were affected by his love of the great, his feeling for the beautiful. He cared for and he advocated what is everywhere purest and finest: Greek art of the most perfect periods, the marbles of Phidias, the frescos of Raphael, the engravings of Marcantonio, the music of Gluck and of Mozart, the poetry of Homer.

As a painter Ingres was no doubt unequal, but he was always admirable in some respect and always a master, even in his faults. Vast compositions were beyond the powers of his imagination, whose fire burned but briefly. It was only with difficulty and after many changes and hesitations that he was able to compose his pictures, but the composition was achieved with a severe taste and a sure touch, and was founded on some tradition carefully chosen and faithfully carried out. His short-breathed genius excelled above all in compositions of only one or two figures, such as 'Œdipus,' 'The Bather,' 'La Source,' 'Venus Anadyomene.'...

Drawing was the strongest point of Ingres' genius, and in it the most diverse qualities are manifested: sometimes it is exquisitely delicate and naïve, sometimes keen and incisive, as in his sketches which are incomparable in what might be called their flavor; sometimes bold, magistral, and striking, sometimes violent and fierce, sometimes suave, tender, and voluptuous.

Color and chiaroscuro were his vulnerable points. His pictures often lack atmosphere, depth, and picturesque quality. The tendency, however, to impart a gray tone to his canvas, the monotony of his palette, was not a mistake of which he was guilty throughout his career. If he did not possess that orchestration of color which was the supreme gift of Eugène Delacroix, he nevertheless shows some charming subtleties and happy variations in his local tones.

Finally, as regards Ingres' touch, it is supple and light, delicate without being thin, expressive and unlabored in his painting of the nude, and exceedingly skilful in the rendering of accessories and of all that calls for elegance in execution. His portraits, notably those of women, are striking proofs of this.

Ingres will live forever because he frequently approaches Raphael in the beauty of his drawing, because, if inferior to Poussin in expression through ordonnance, he is sometimes his superior in expression through gesture, as also in his search for and attainment of beauty. And he will live because he has rivaled Holbein in portraiture, surpassed David in style, equaled Prud'hon in grace, and created certain forms which in their grandeur seem to be descended from the frescos of Michelangelo. Yes, whatever may be the inconstancy of fame, whatever may be the ideas which are to govern future generations, it may be affirmed that Jean-Auguste-Dominique Ingres will never be deposed from the place which he won by a hard struggle, by the force of his genius – a place that is not only on a plane with the painters who have given luster to the French school, but near those who have been the glory of the Renaissance. – ABRIDGED FROM THE FRENCH

HENRY LAPAUZE

'MÉLANGES SUR L'ART FRANÇAIS'

The term "realist," as applied to Ingres, requires explanation, for since his day times have changed, and we now rank him among the idealists, or, to speak more correctly, among the classicists. Certain Philistines would even go so far as to accuse him of being bound down to a formula; that is to say, of being conventional in his manner of painting, although this was the very thing against which he rebelled so vehemently in David.

Now, it is not simply by contrast with that pompous, declamatory, formal, and frigid painter against whom he revolted, that Ingres is a realist, but because he actually did draw his inspiration from reality, because he infused into his work the breath of life. His seeming coldness arises from the fact that it was through line alone that he sought for expression, reducing color to a subordinate rôle. The uniformity of which he is accused, as if he had made use of some one established mold, springs from the loftiness of his style. But his drawing, like his style, even in attaining the very acme of natural beauty, never deviates from the domain of truth, and invariably derives its inspiration from life itself. This is the case even with those celebrated canvases from which he seems to have voluntarily excluded all soul, in order that its everlasting restlessness, its turmoil, and its passion should not disarrange the grand harmony of the composition, those canvases in which his brush-work has the sharp precision of a chisel, and in which his art resembles sculpture almost more than painting. Even in these works, notwithstanding the superficial aspect of rigidity and immobility which strikes the eye, there is perceptible a conscientious submission to nature, and to truth.

It was voluntarily and for a definite esthetic end that Ingres eliminated movement and color, so that line and attitude – in other words, all that which in human beauty least stirs the emotions and appeals most directly to the mind – might reign supreme. "Serenity," he used to say, "is to the body what wisdom is to the soul." Color possesses in itself resources which he despised as if they had been shams. To compose a picture for effect, to select some ingenious or powerful motive and offset it by a symphony of tones, seemed to him beneath the dignity of art. That is why he denounced Delacroix.

To make use of light in a similar way, to dazzle the eye by astonishing effects of chiaroscuro, to bewilder the sight as an orchestra stuns the ear with the clangor of its brass, by breaking black shadows with vivid lights, was in his opinion artistic disloyalty. That is why he placed but a low estimate upon Rembrandt.

To use color as if it were something plastic, to paint with what is called a "full brush," with exaggerated high lights, loaded paint, glazings, and visible brush-strokes, was to him blasphemous. That is why he did not assign a high rank to the Venetians – with the exception of Titian.

To animate painting by qualities purely sensual, to make a lavish display of the gorgeous splendor of brilliant stuffs, rich brocades and velvets, and gold and silver plate, to paint in glowing rosy hues and amid voluptuous surroundings the plumpness of naked flesh, aroused his indignation and his repugnance as if such art were a desecration. That is why he held Rubens in abhorrence. "There is something of the butcher in that painter," he used to say; "his flesh is like fresh meat, and his setting like a butcher's stall."

Such was the force of Ingres' convictions, such the rigorous decrees of his conscience in regard to what he considered the good and the evil in painting, that his violent antipathies were not confined to a man's work, but extended to the man himself, even were he no longer living. "You are my pupils," he would say to the young artists working under him, "therefore you are my friends, and as such you would not bow to one of my enemies were he to pass along the street. Turn away, then, from Rubens whenever you meet him in the galleries, for if you approach him he will be sure to speak evil to you of my teaching and of me."

Going one day before the opening of the Exposition of 1855 into the room especially reserved for his works, and to which the public had not yet been admitted, he suspected that the keeper, in disobedience to orders, had just allowed Delacroix to enter. "Some one has been in here," he cried; "the room smells of brimstone!"

In sacrificing color to line, the charm of light to the eloquence of form, the pleasure of the eye to the enjoyment of the mind, the sensual delight of the palette to the intellectual enjoyment of style, Ingres realized a great ideal, founded as much, perhaps, upon the absence of certain qualities as upon the triumphant presence of certain others. His temperament, so restrained in his color, is revealed in his nervous, vigorous drawing. It is evident from the valuable studies preserved in the Museum of Montauban what tremendous struggles he underwent when he took his pencil in hand. What efforts, what will-power! What frankness and boldness of execution, and what scrupulous conscientiousness in his repeated attempts! There were times when he would weep in utter despair. "I can no longer draw!" he would lament, even at the time when he was at the head of the French school. Color never caused him such agony. He never worried his head about that; it was sure to come, sober and subdued, following the drawing like a docile slave whose duty it is to escort his master, to keep step with him, but at a respectful distance. No great draftsman, he declared, could ever fail to find the color that would best suit the character of his drawing. And again, he said, "I shall write over the door of my studio, 'School of Drawing,' and I shall make painters."...

It has been said of Ingres that he was a Greek who had strayed from antiquity into our own times. We know, however, that nature does not produce geniuses at haphazard, but that every great creator expresses the thoughts, ideas, and aspirations of his time. Ingres was no exception to this law. Not only was he the child of his century, but he was its representative, both in the classic reaction and the romantic impulse; and as in his well-balanced mind the two tendencies were modified one by the other, the result was this great and harmonious genius which is on a plane superior to the feelings and passions of his epoch, into which, nevertheless, his intrepid spirit boldly plunged. – FROM THE FRENCH

RICHARD MUTHER

'THE HISTORY OF MODERN PAINTING'

I doubt whether up to the present time any one has rightly understood the mysterious figure of Ingres, of the man who in his youth was enraptured by "the spirit, the grace, the originality of Watteau and the delicious color of his pictures," and who, at a later time, not because of incapacity, but out of deliberate intention, introduced discords of color into his paintings; of this classicist *par excellence*, who is counted among the greatest artists, in the familiar and graceful style, who are recorded in the history of art.

Like David, Ingres has survived as a portrait-painter only. Like him, when he found himself face to face with nature, he relented, and forgot the strict system which he had elaborated for his great pictures. He has painted portraits which imprint themselves on the memory like medals, struck in metallic sharpness. Here too he is unequal, often cold and commonplace, but more frequently quite admirable. In these paintings, cast as it were in bronze, there is something that comes from the fresh original source of all art; they have that vein of realism by which the vigorous idealism of Raphael is distinguished from the conventional idealism of a professor of historical painting. Here one finds real treasures, creations of remarkable vital power, and in admirable taste. They show that Ingres, apparently so systematic, had a profound love for living nature, and they insure the immortality of his name. His historical pictures are works which compel our esteem, but his portraits are splendid creations which can truly stand comparison with the great old masters....

In Holbein's portraits the whole German community of his time has been handed down to us; in those of Van Dyck, the aristocracy of England under Charles i. So also Ingres has depicted for us, with all its failings and all its virtues, the middle-class hierarchy of Louis Philippe's reign, which felt itself to be the first estate, the summit of the nation, felt sure of the morrow, was proud of itself, of its intelligence and energy, which pursued with correctness its moral course of life, revered order and hated all excess – including that of the colorists. It is this same spirit which animated Ingres himself, that splendid *"bourgeois"* of art. His portrait of Bertin is justly his most celebrated work; not merely the painted petrifaction of a newspaper potentate, but also one of those portraits which bring a whole epoch home to one's mind....

But however highly one must estimate the importance of such a work, Ingres is nevertheless at his highest, not in his *painted* likenesses, but in his portrait-drawings. In the former the raw colors are still, at times, offensive. The faces sometimes have the conventional, uniform coloring of his historical pictures, the historical tone. Almost always the flesh looks like wood, the dress like metal, blue robes like steel. His drawings, however, are to be admired without criticism. Ingres lived in his youth, at Rome, as a drawer of portraits. For eight *scudi* he did the bust, for twelve the whole figure, raging inwardly the while at being kept from "great art" by such journeyman-work.

In these pieces an artistic eye which was now inexorable, now tender and full of fancy, has looked on nature, and, in flowing pencil-strokes, has caught with spirit and with the certain touch of direct feeling the real fulness of life in what he saw. These drawings show that "Father Ingres" possessed not only a highly cultivated intelligence and iron strength of will, not only the genius of industry, but also a heart, a genuine, warm, and fine-feeling heart; that he was in his innermost being by no means the cold academician, the stiff doctrinaire, which he appears to be in his large pictures, and which his opposition to the romantic school made of him. Here we have a charmer such as the Primitives were, a charmer such as the Impressionists are, like Massys and Manet, like Dürer and Degas, like all who have looked nature in the face. And while these drawings, at once occasional and austere, place him as a draftsman on a level with the greatest masters in the history of art, they also show him, the reactionary, as at the same time a man of progress, as the connecting link between the great art of the first half and the familiar art which rules over the second half of the nineteenth century.

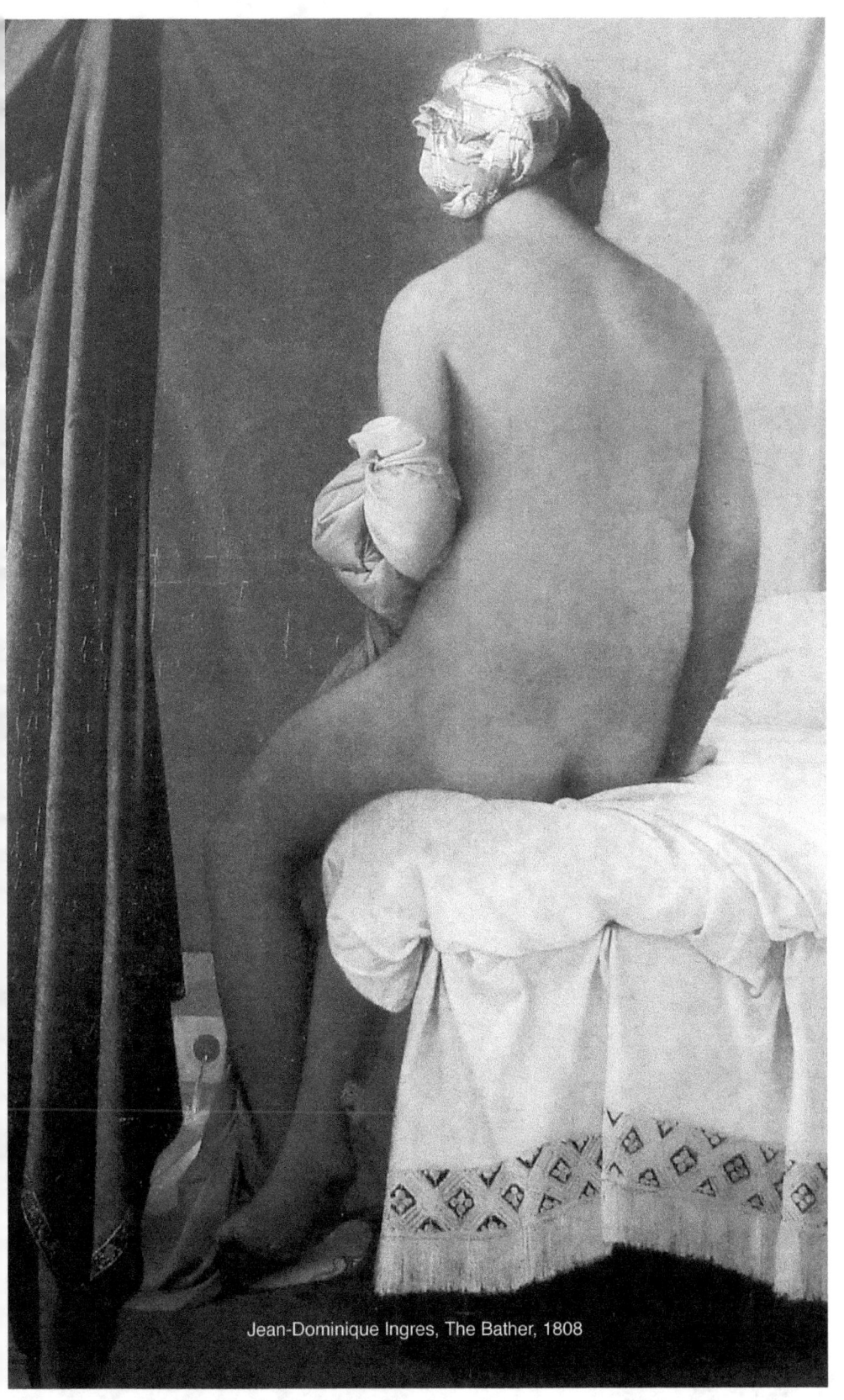
Jean-Dominique Ingres, The Bather, 1808

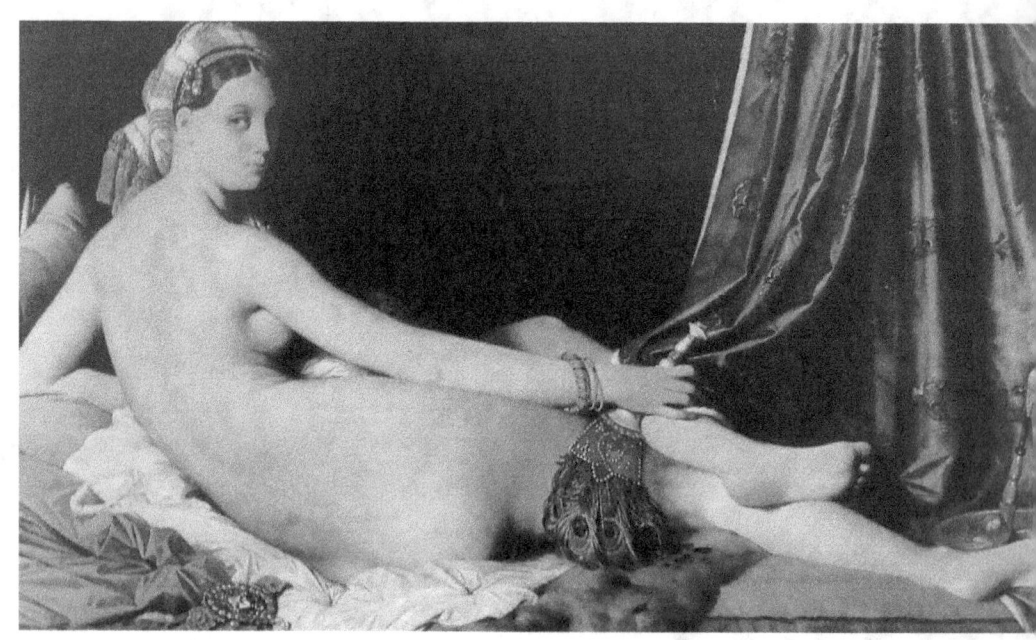

Jean-Dominique Ingres, Grand Odalisque, 1814

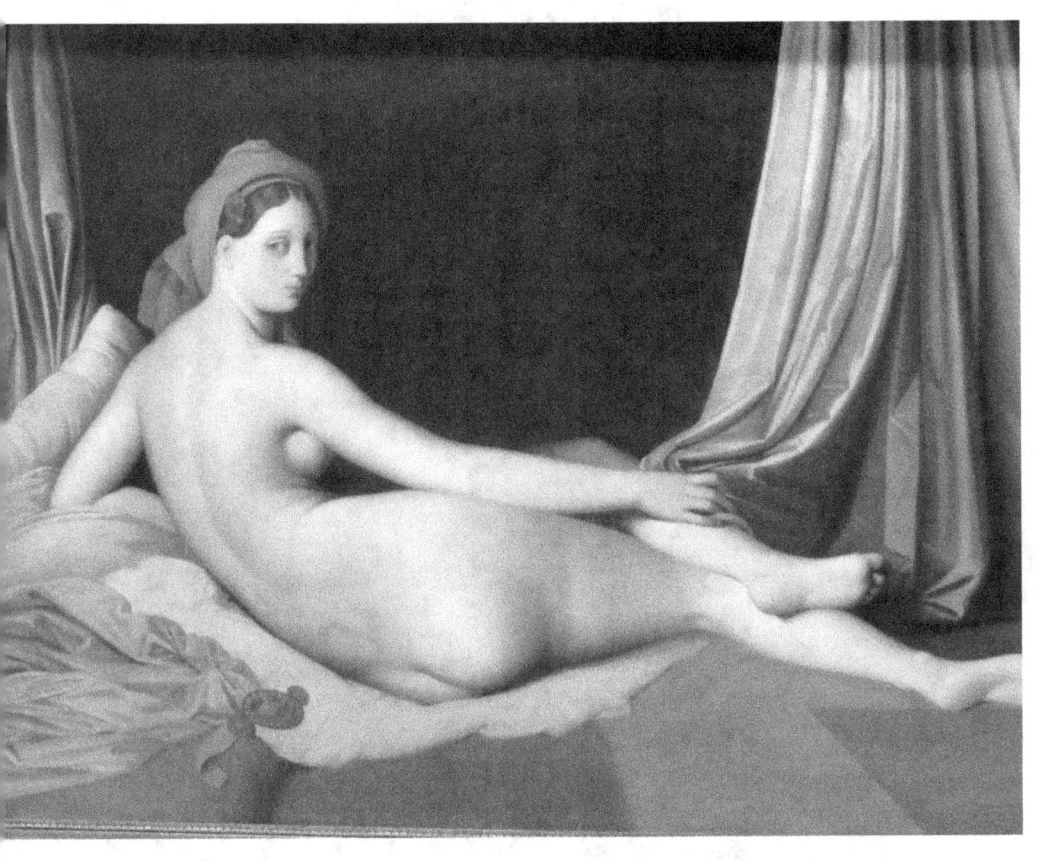

J.A.D. Ingres, Odalisque, Metropolitan Museum of Art

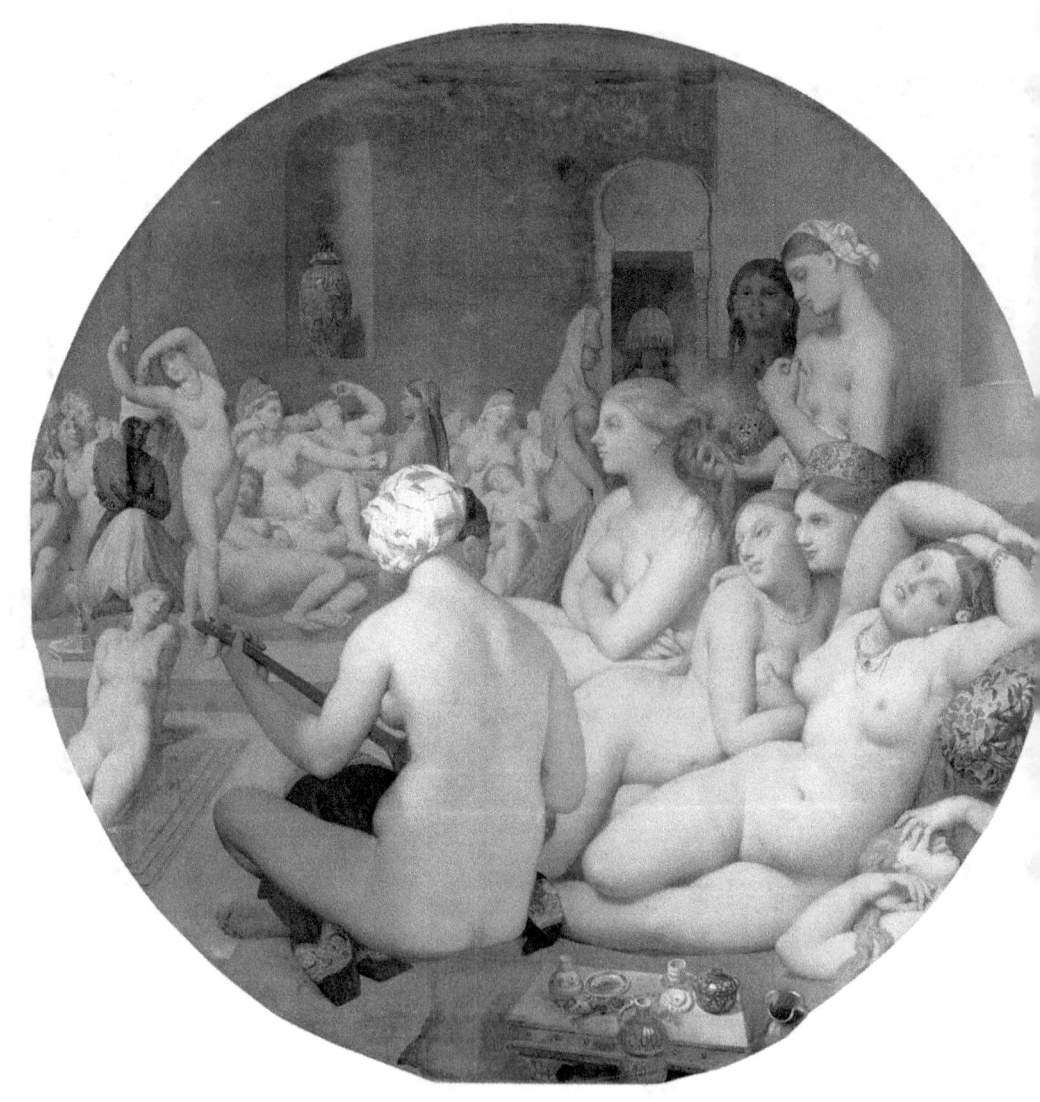

J.A.D. Ingres, Turkish Bath, 1862, Louvre

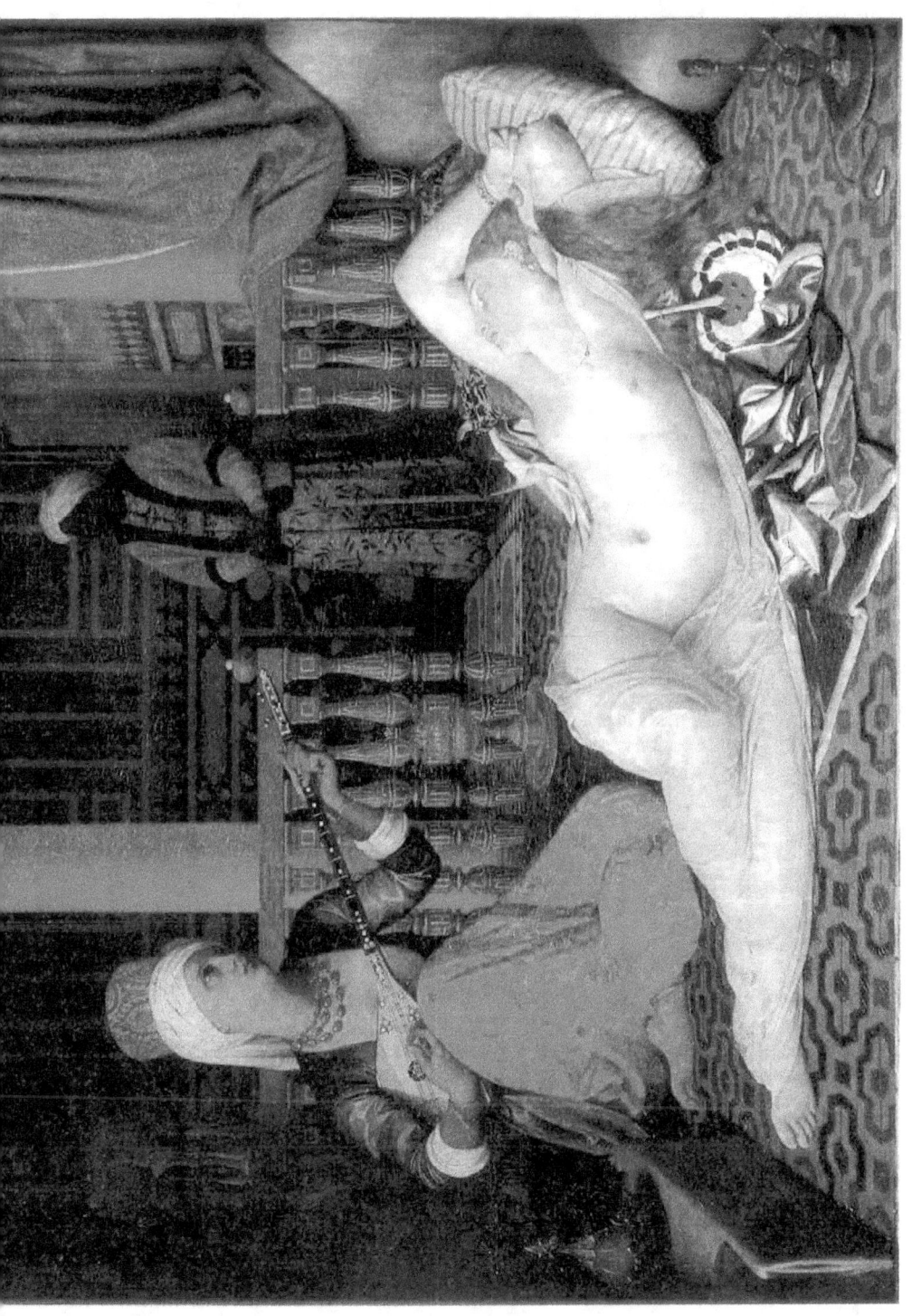

Jean-Dominique Ingres, Odalisque

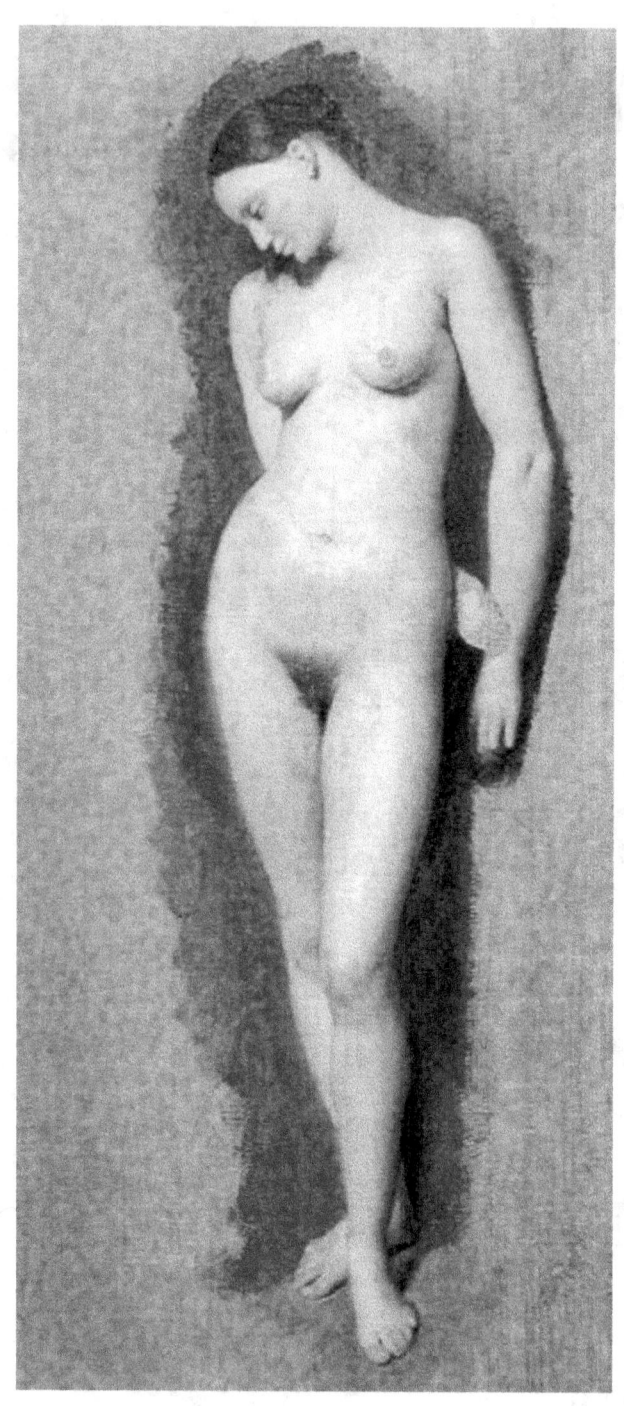

Jean-Dominique Ingres, Nude Study

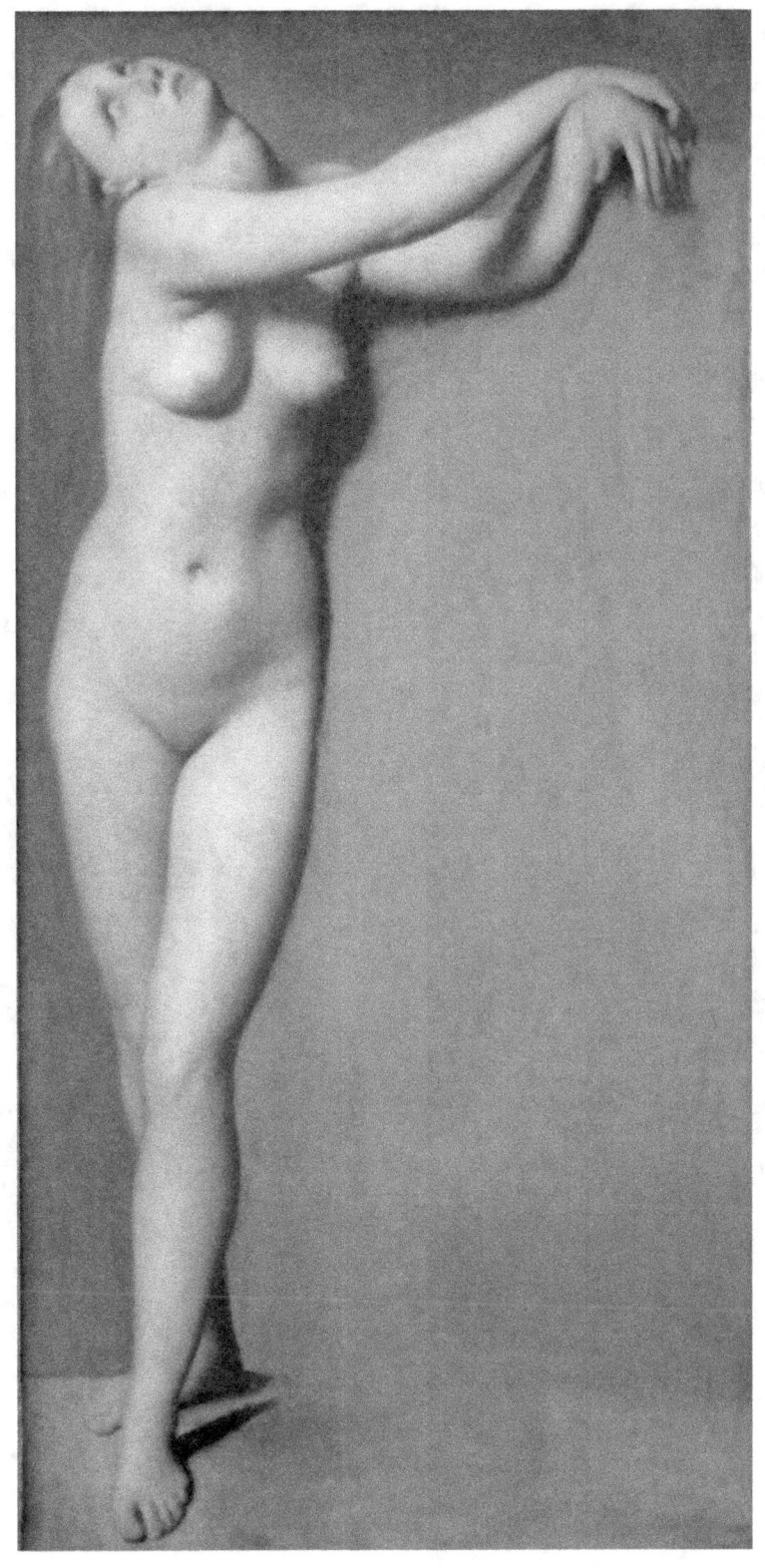

J.A.D. Ingres, study for Ruggiero

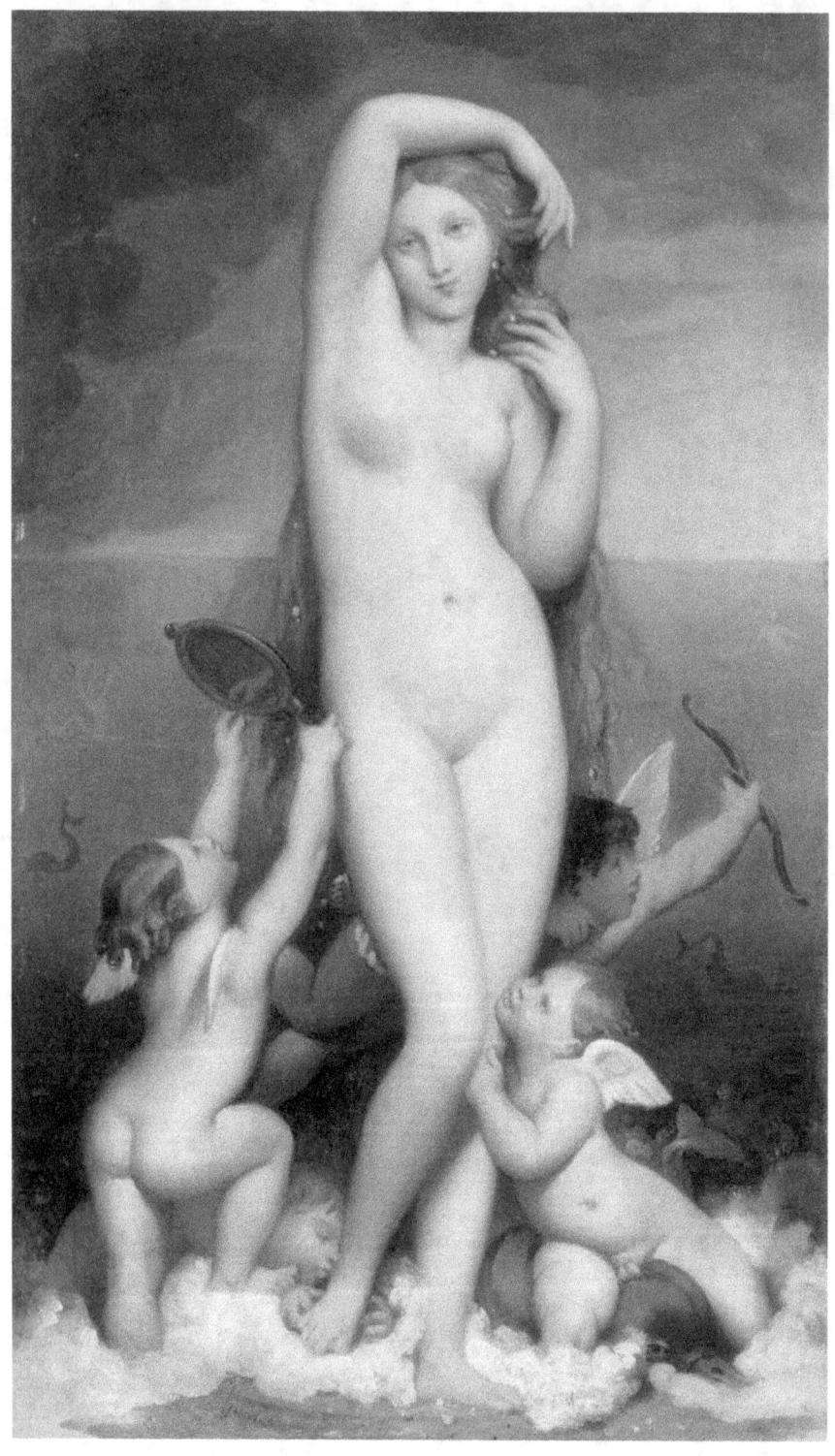

J.A.D. Ingres, Venus Anadyomène, 1825-50, Paris

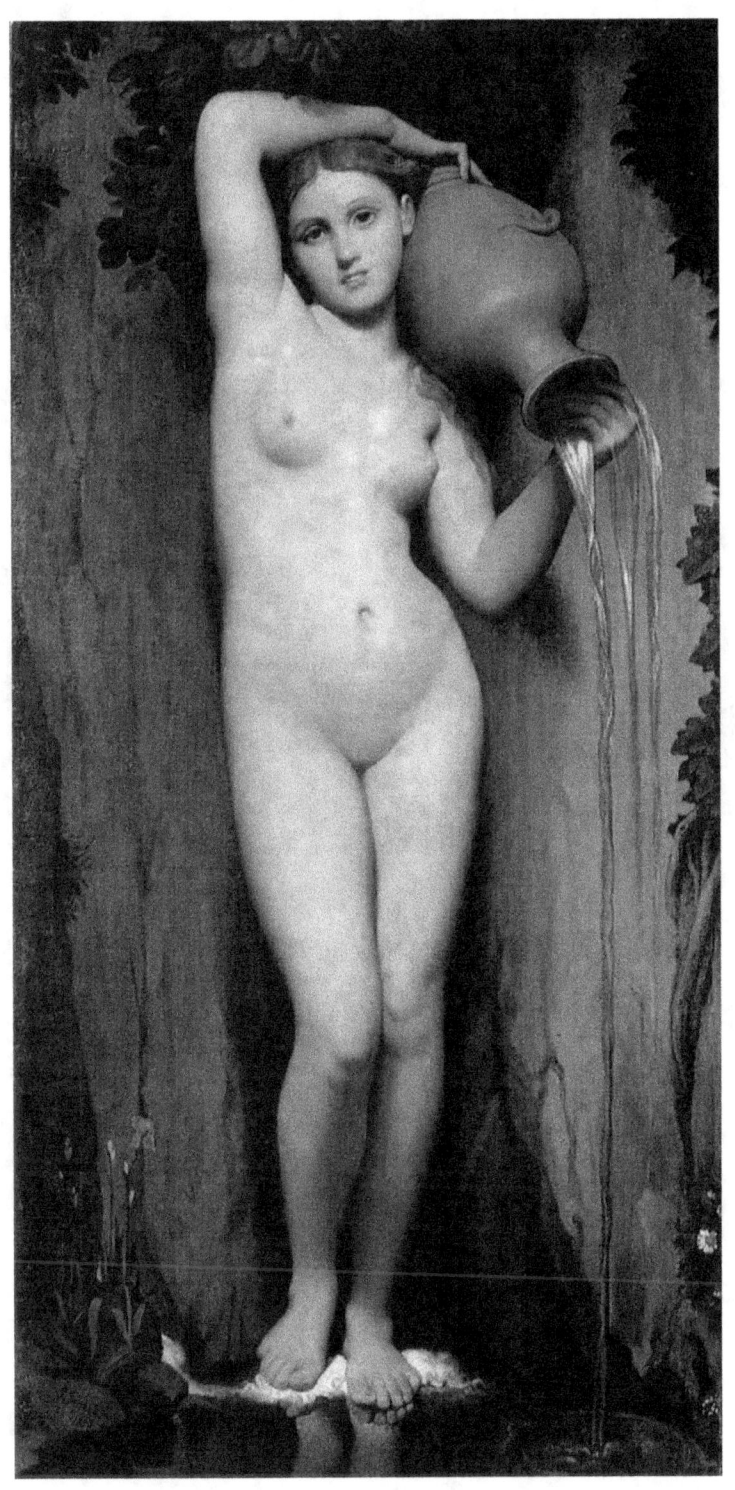

J.A.D.Ingres, The Source, 1856, Paris

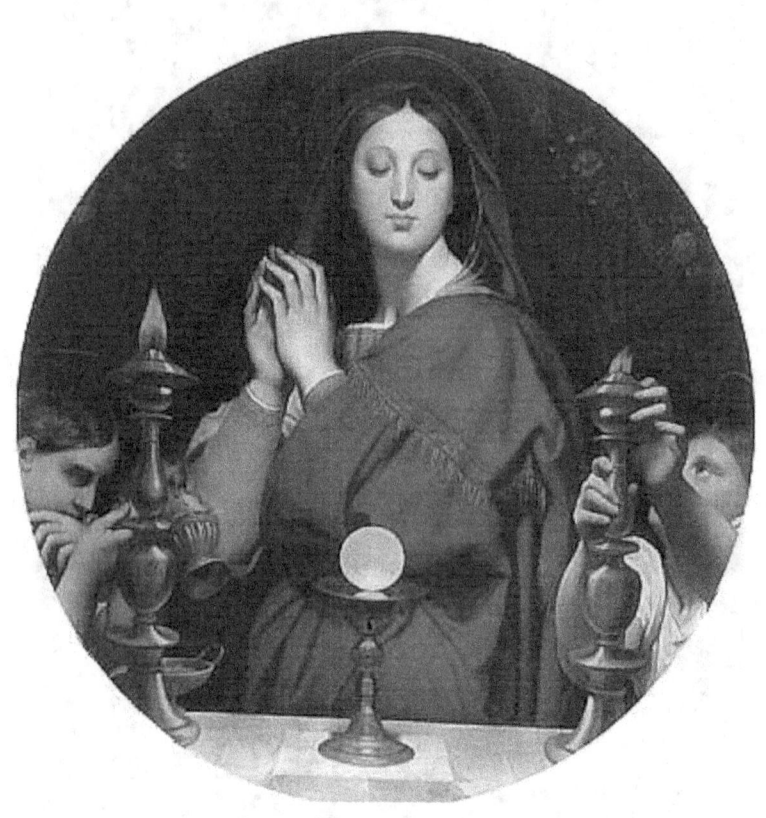

J.A.D. Ingres, The Virgin of the Host, 1852,
Metropolitan Museum of Art

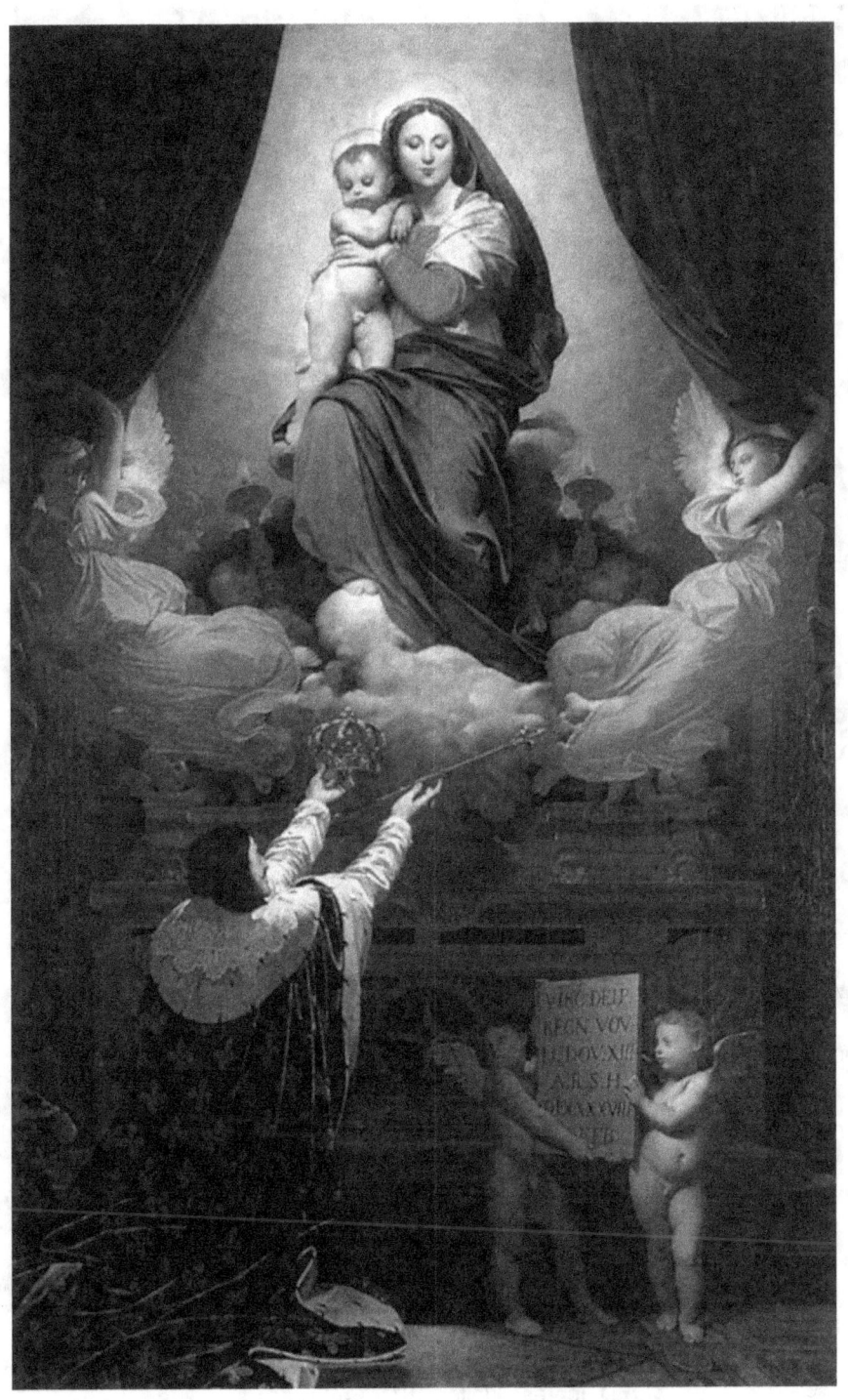

J.A.D. Ingres, O Voto de Luis XIII, 1824, Montauban

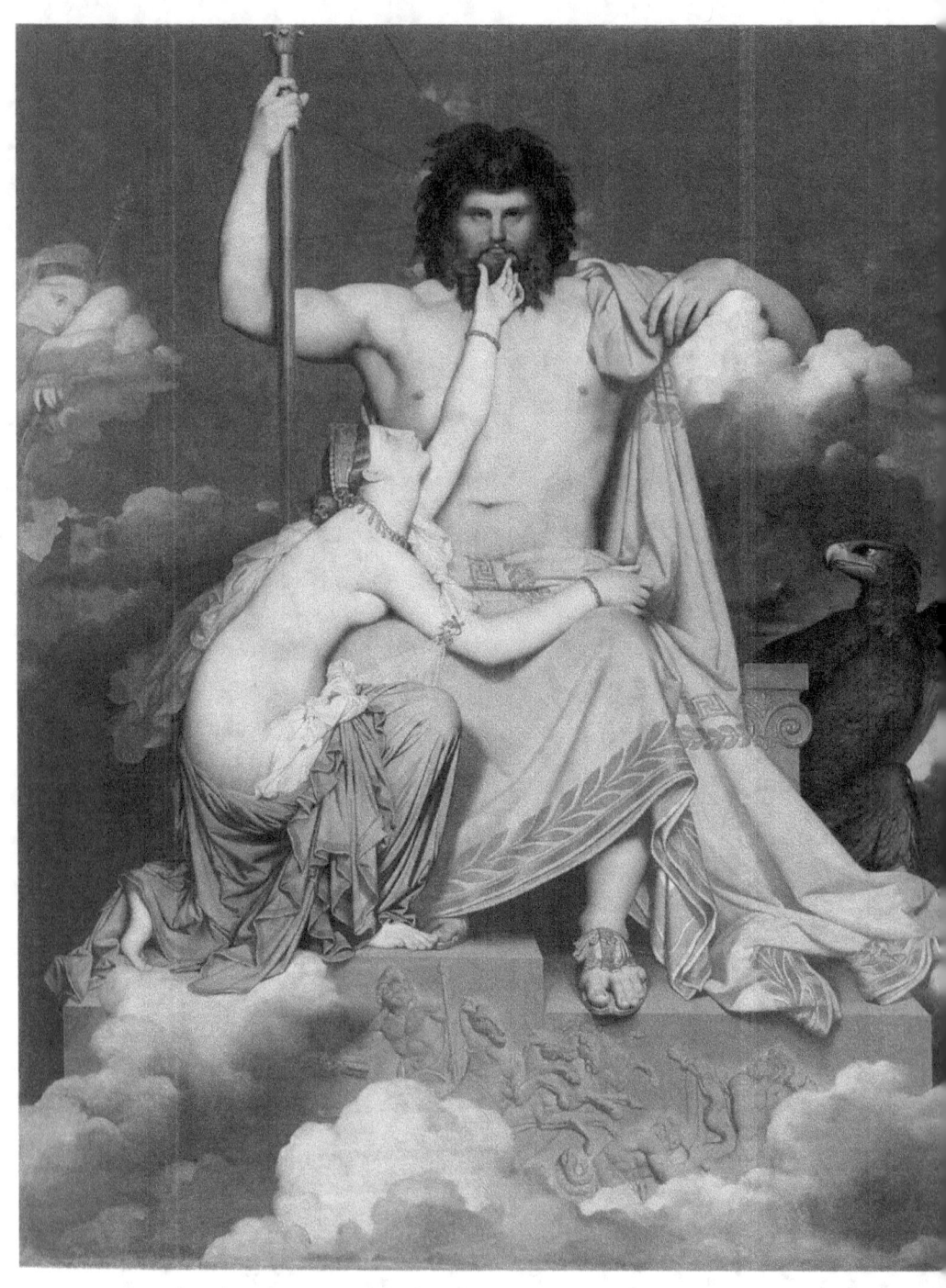

J.A.D. Ingres, Jupiter, 1811, Provence

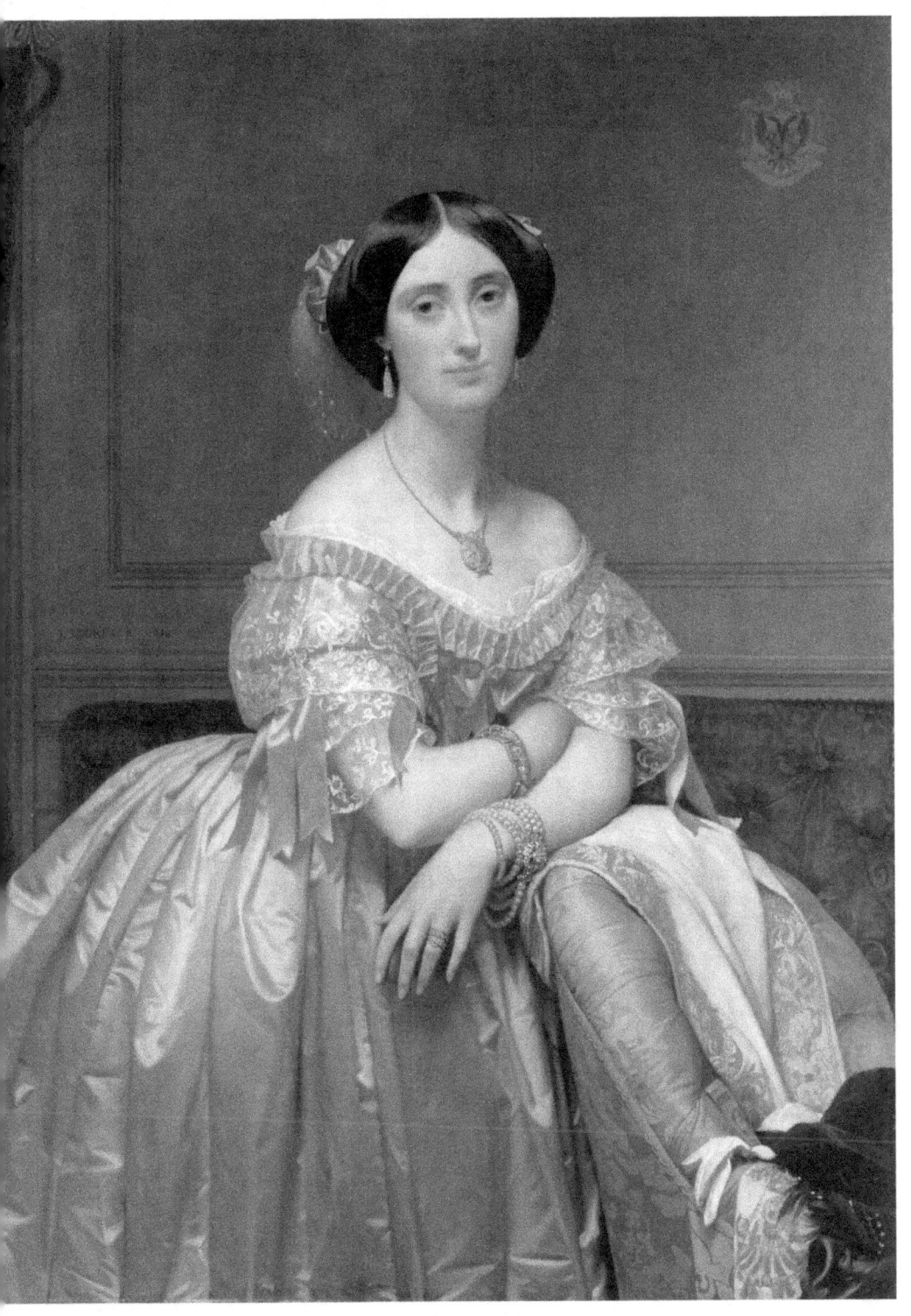

J.A.D.Ingres, Princesse Albert de Broglie, 1853, New York

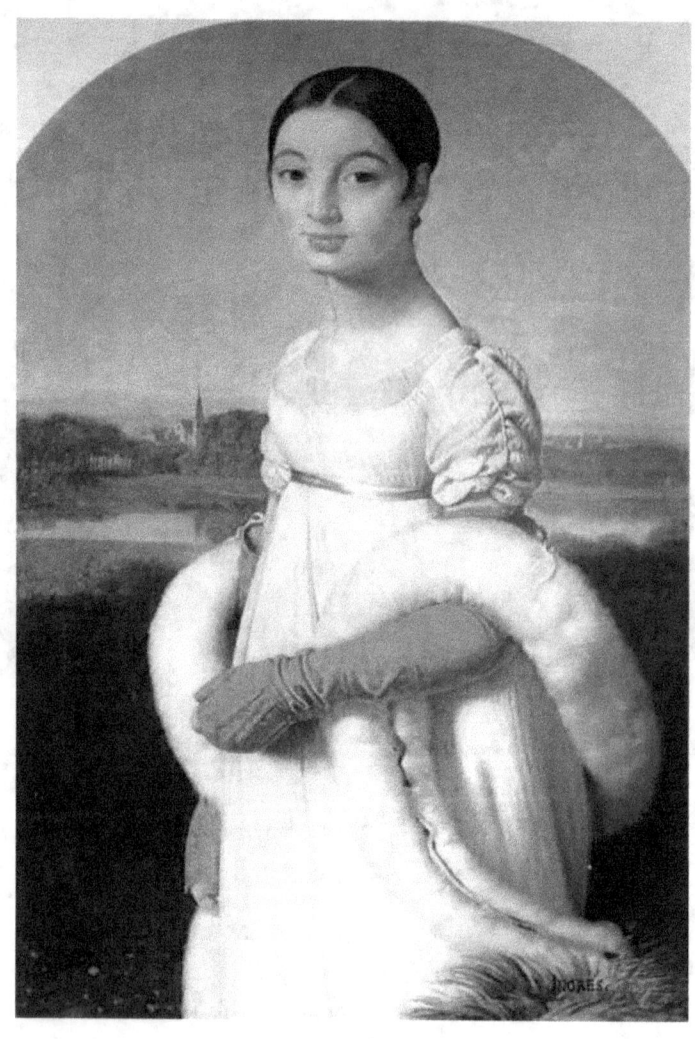

J.A.D. Ingres, Mademoiselle Riviere, 1805, Louvre

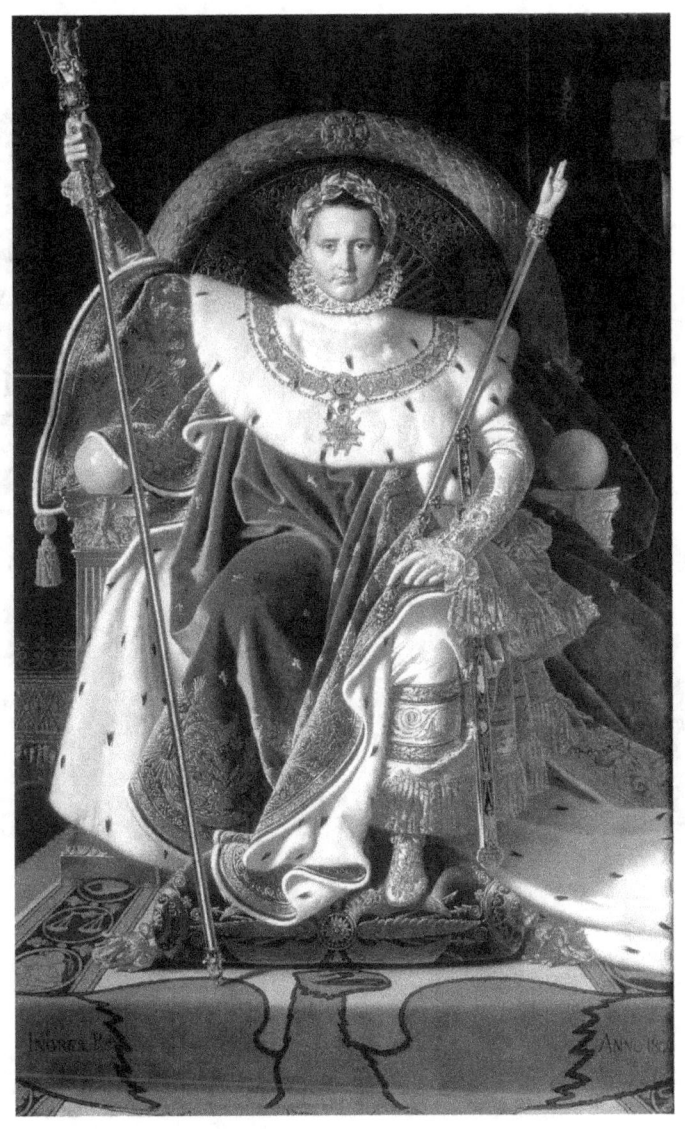

J.A.D. Ingres, Napoleon, 1806, Paris

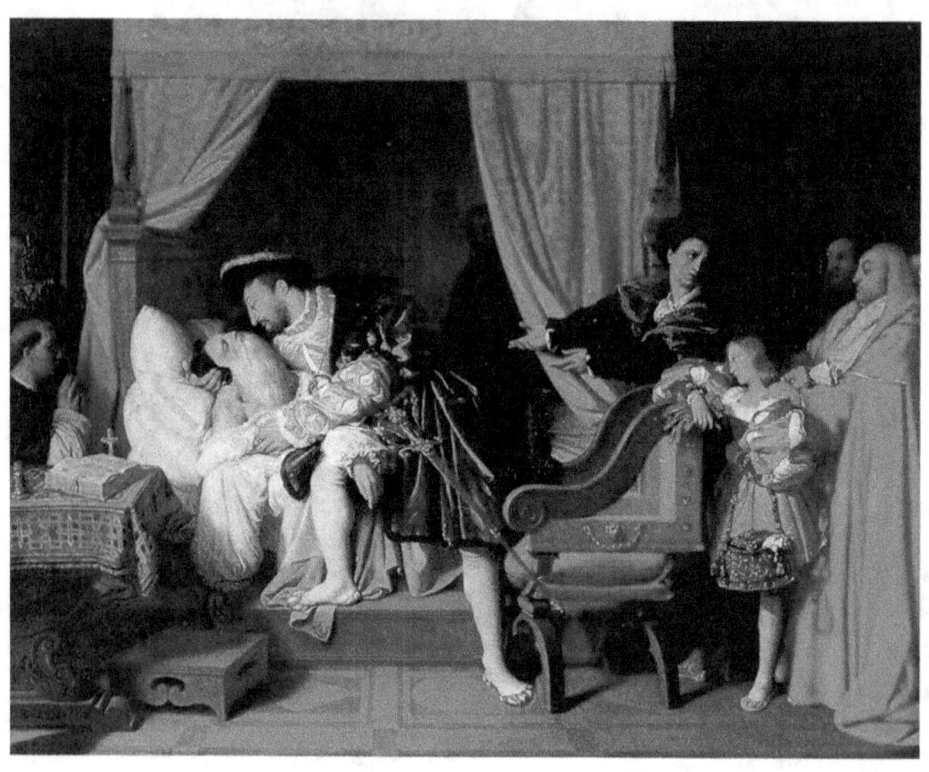

J.A.D. Ingres, The Death of Leonardo, 1818

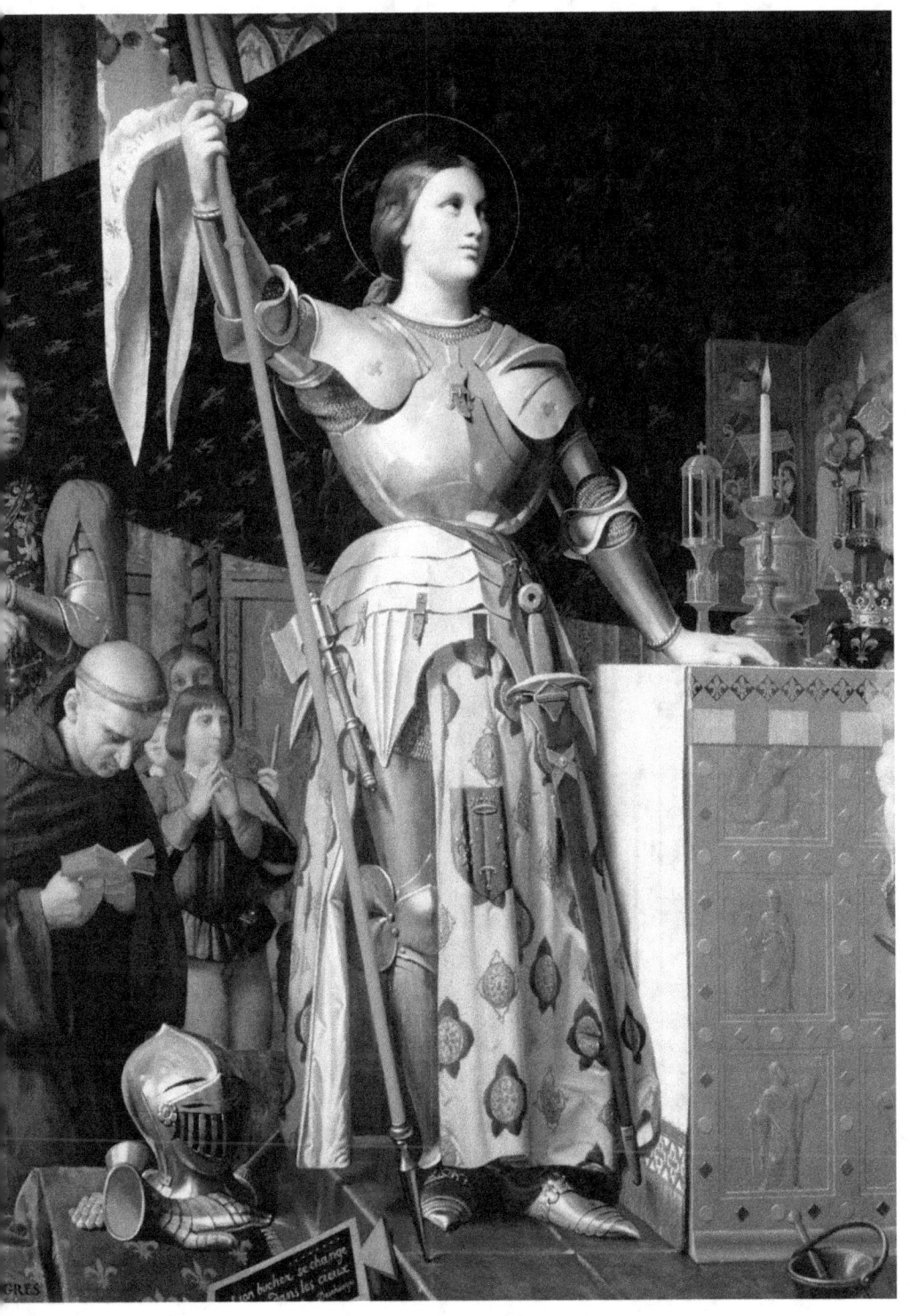

J.A.D. Ingres, The Coronation of Charles VII, Joan of Arc, 1854, Louvre

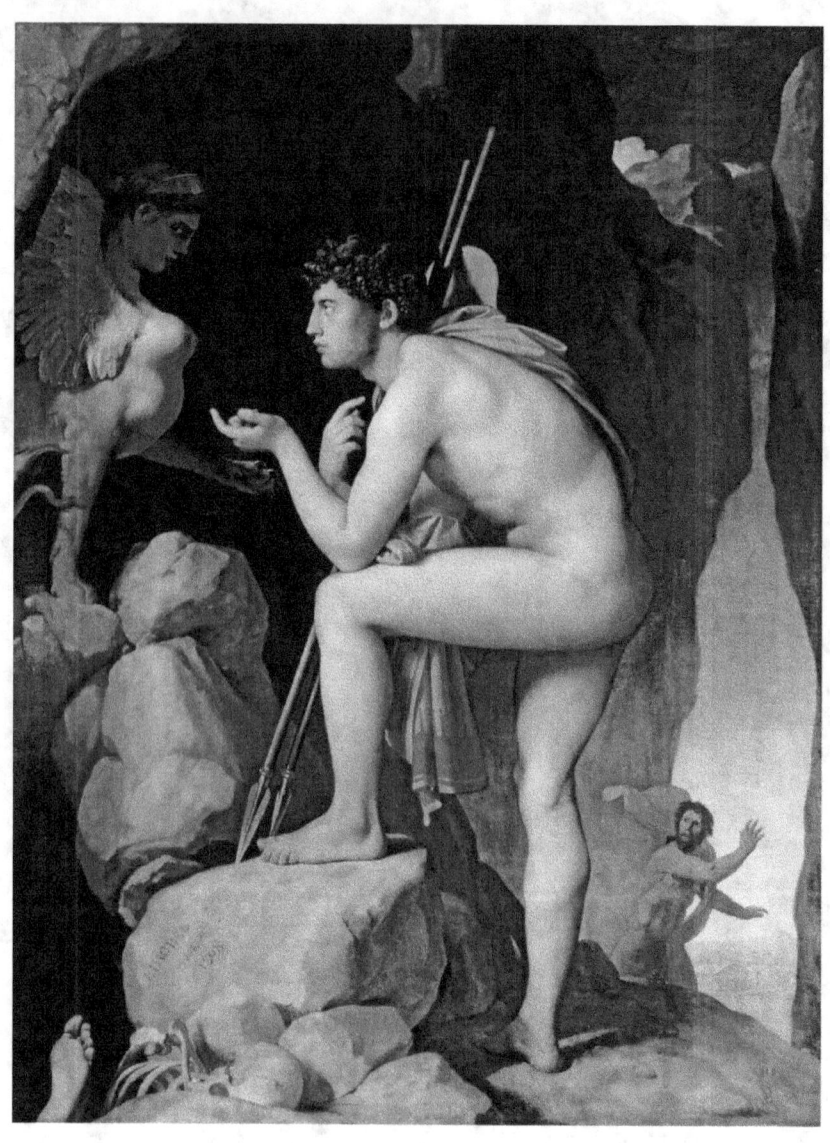

J.A.D.Ingres, Oedipus and the Sphinx, 1807, Louvre, Paris

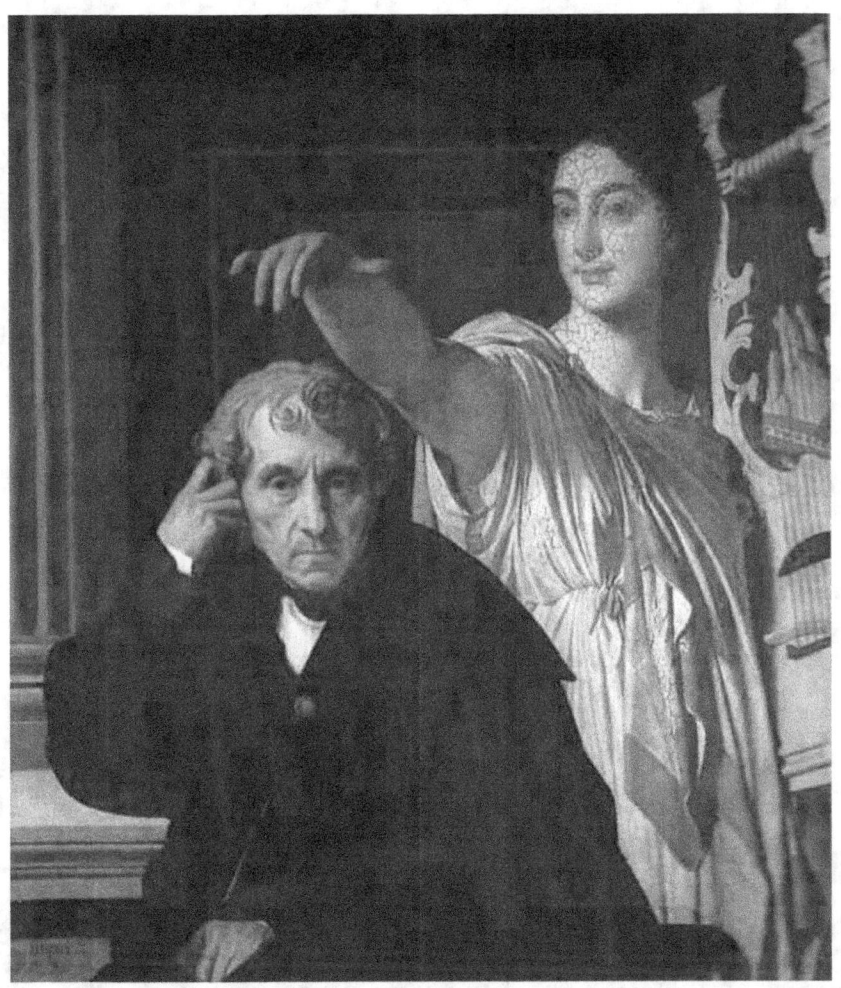

J.A.D. Ingres, Luigi Cherubini and the Muse of Lyric Poetry, 1842, Louvre

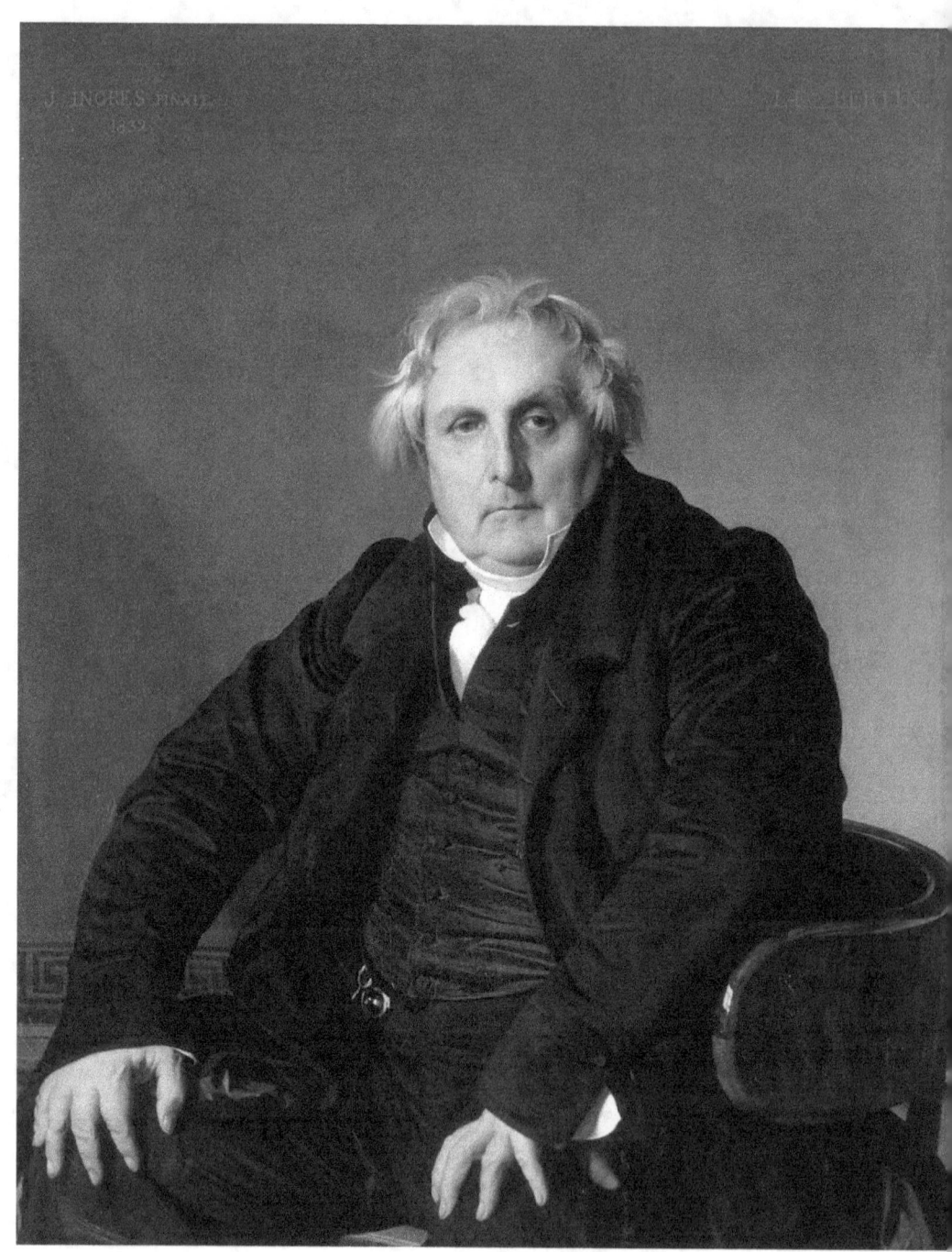

J.A.D. Ingres, Louis-Francois Bertin, 1832, Louvre

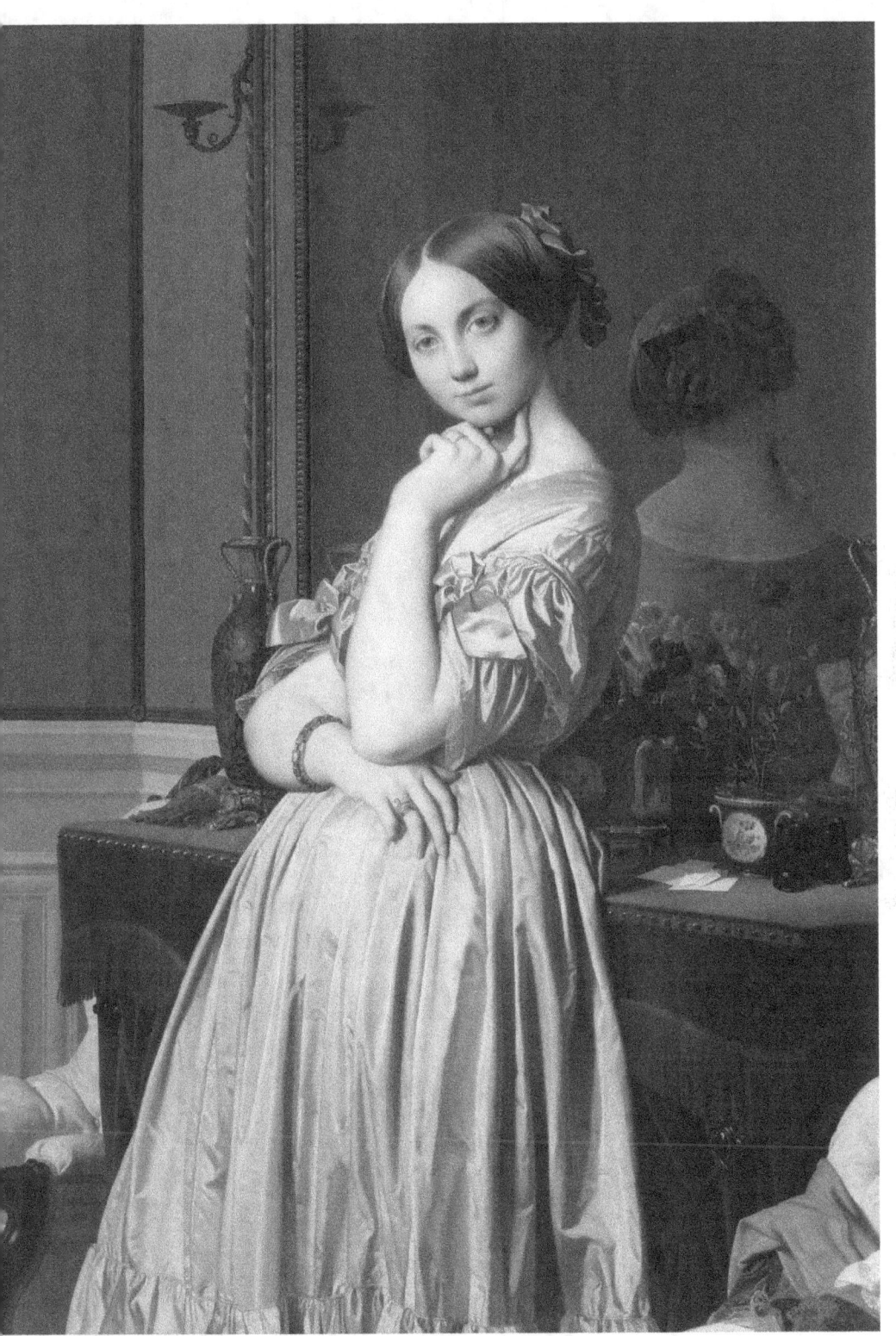

J.A.D. Ingres, Comtesse d'Haussonville, 1845, Frick Collection
(this page and over)

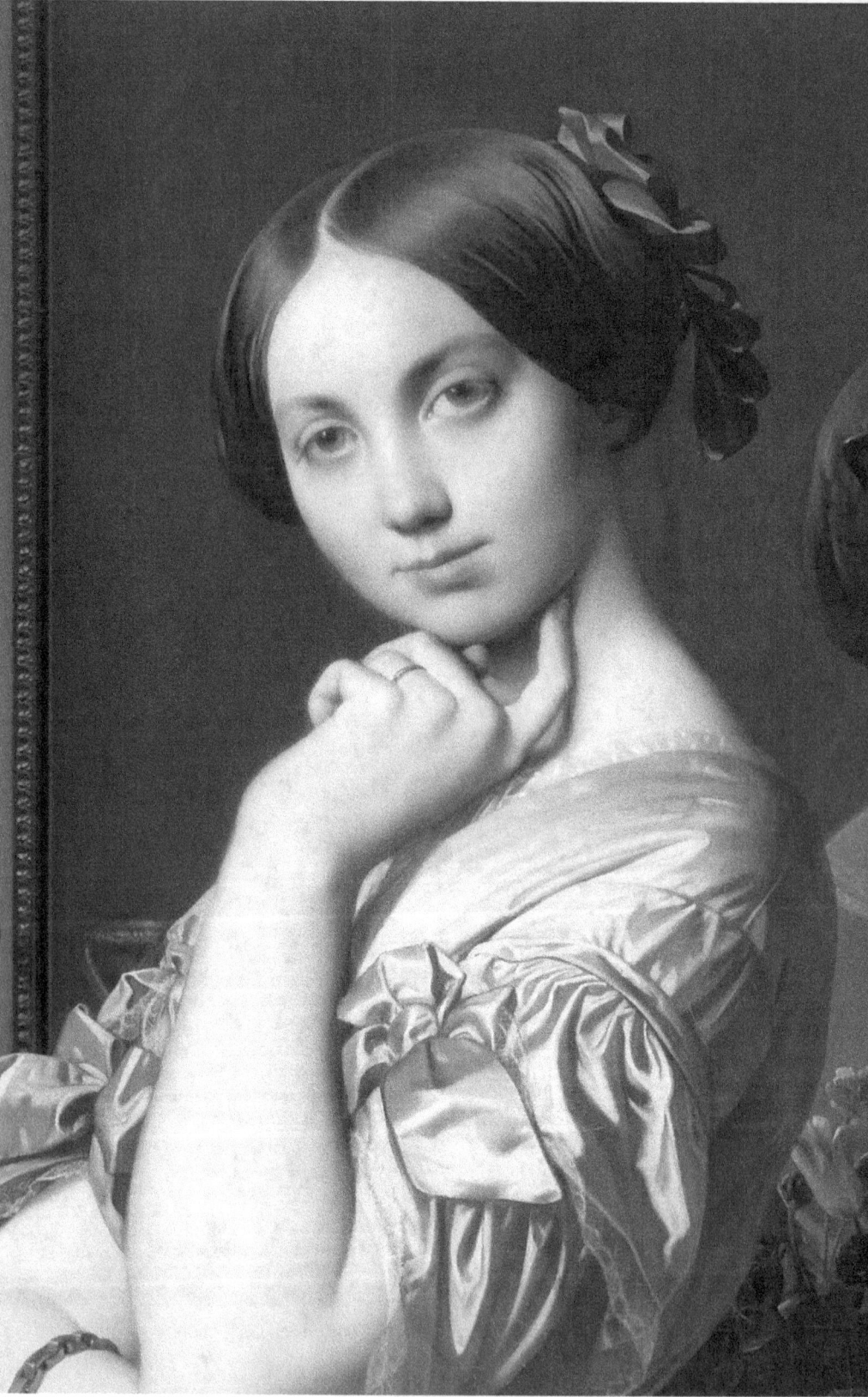

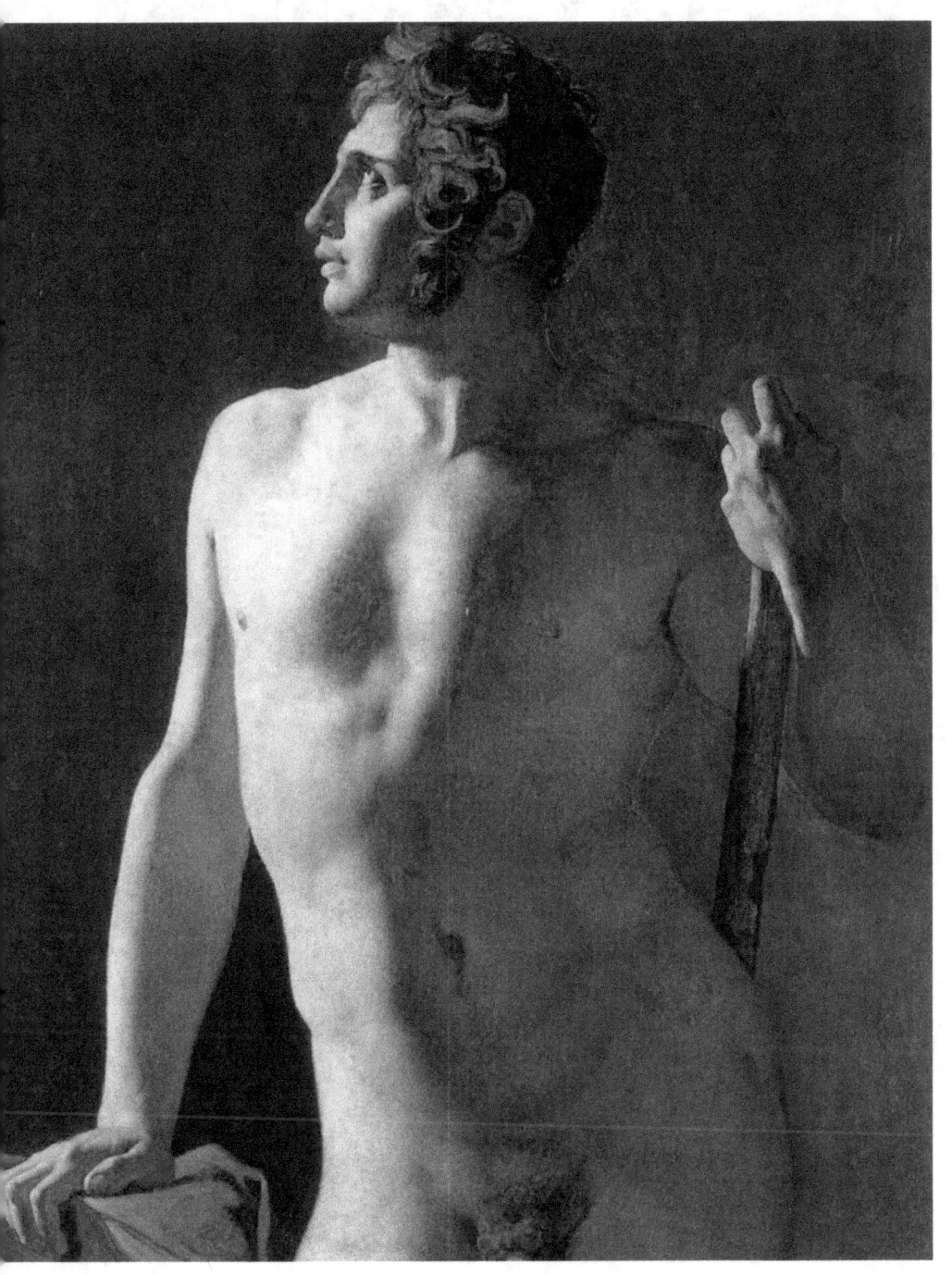

J.A.D. Ingres, Study of a Male Nude, 1801

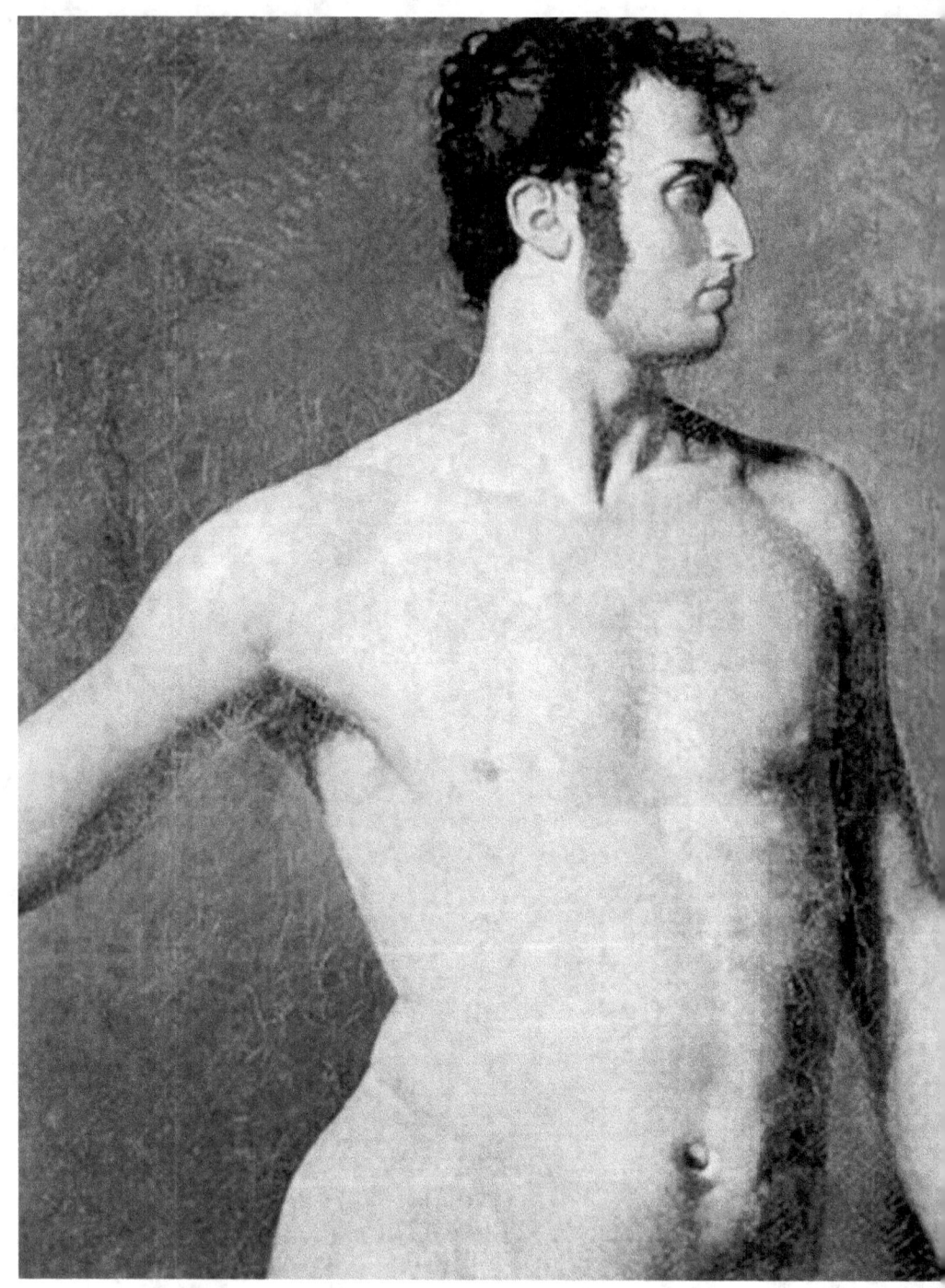

J.A.D. Ingres, Male Torso, 1801, Musée Ingres

THE WORKS OF INGRES

DESCRIPTIONS OF THE PLATES

PORTRAIT OF INGRES BY HIMSELF
UFFIZI GALLERY, FLORENCE

This portrait was painted when Ingres was seventy-five. He has been described at that time as strong and vigorous, short of stature, thick-set, and ill-proportioned. His complexion was sallow, his cheek-bones prominent, his eyes dark and keen, his eyebrows slight and contracted in a frown, his nose seemingly short because of the great length of his upper lip. His hair was short and stiff, and worn parted like a woman's. His appearance, it was said, suggested a retired man of business, or a curate in citizen's clothes, rather than an artist with whom the love of beauty amounted to a passion.

'ŒDIPUS AND THE SPHINX'

During the second year of his sojourn in Rome, Ingres produced his famous picture of 'Œdipus and the Sphinx,' in which his individual manner of conception and execution was first affirmed. The mythical hero is here represented, not as David would have represented him, cold and lifeless as a statue, but as a man endowed with the beauty of a Greek athlete rather than a god, and although his body is drawn and modeled with such academic exactitude that its very perfection is in itself somewhat wearisome, yet when compared with the creations of the painter of the Horatii and the Sabines, it can readily be seen why Ingres, pure classicist though he be, should have been regarded in his own day as a revolutionary.

The old Greek legend is here portrayed of Œdipus explaining the riddle of the Sphinx, whereby he delivered Thebes from the cruelties of that monster who had mercilessly destroyed every man who had failed to solve her riddle. Œdipus has entered the cave in which the Sphinx is seated. With one foot placed upon a rock and his elbow resting on his knee, he gazes intently in her face as he explains that a being with four feet, two feet, and three feet is man, who, in infancy, crawls upon all fours, in manhood stands erect upon two feet, and in old age supports his tottering legs with a staff.

A red mantle is thrown over the young Greek's shoulder, against which rest two spears, weapons with which to defend himself if need be against the attack of the dreaded Sphinx. The bones and portions of the bodies of the creature's victims lie scattered about, and in the distance a man is seen flying in terror.

The canvas is now in the Louvre. It measures about six feet high by four feet ten inches wide.

'PORTRAIT OF MADAME DE SENONNES'

"In the portrait of Madame de Senonnes, now in the Museum of Nantes," writes M. Louis Gonse, "Ingres stands unrivaled. Look carefully at the illusive serenity of this strange face where no brush-stroke is visible, at the vague, fleeting smile of the parted lips, the smooth, lustrous hair, the throat modeled like an alabaster column, the sinuous lines of the body, the beautiful, large, plump hands loaded with rings; observe the perfect nonchalance of the pose, and then see the reflection of the back of the head in the mirror – a favorite device of the Primitives; note the wonderful values of the garnet red of the dress against the silky yellow cushions with their reddish brown tones, the marvelous way in which the cashmere shawl and lace ruff are painted, the strong and harmonious color-scheme based on the play of complementary tones, all the sharp precision of the drawing, carried as it is to the utmost limits, and then say whether in all modern painting there is another work which combines such a variety of perfections. This portrait of Madame de Senonnes is to Ingres' portraits of women what the one of Monsieur Bertin is to his portraits of men.

"A visiting-card stuck into the frame of the mirror, with the inscription '*Ing. Roma*,' tells us that the picture was painted in the eternal city – apparently between 1806 and 1810. According to report, Ingres had a tender feeling for this fair Roman model, who, child of the people as she was, had lately become the wife of the Vicomte de Senonnes. And in truth, he has put into this portrait all the ardor, all the conviction, of his genius.

"Madame de Senonnes died young; and the vicomte, returning from Italy to his home in Angers, married again, on which occasion he presented this portrait to his brother, who promptly relegated it to the attic. At the brother's death his heirs sold it for one hundred and twenty francs ($24.00) to a dealer who afterwards offered it to the Museum of Nantes, which unhesitatingly gave him the sum of four thousand francs ($800.00) for it. To-day it would bring, at the lowest estimate, one hundred thousand francs, and the time will undoubtedly come when it will be valued at a million."

'MONSIEUR LEBLANC' (DRAWING)

"Ingres' portraits in lead-pencil," writes M. Henry Lapauze, "are the most remarkable, if indeed they might not be called the greatest, productions of his genius.... In them we find unquestionably that quality of realism, over-conscientious, perhaps, but devoid of all coarseness, and that power of imparting life which in his large paintings is more or less concealed beneath the formality of his style."

The drawing reproduced in plate iii, and now in the Bonnat Collection at Bayonne, was made in Florence in 1822, as a preparatory study for a portrait in oil, executed in the following year. Drawn with a sureness of touch, a breadth, simplicity, and freedom, and at the same time a scrupulous precision, every line is significant. Monsieur Leblanc himself, dressed according to the fashion of the day in high silk hat and ample cloak, seems to stand before us in miniature.

'MADAME DESTOUCHE' (DRAWING)

"The drawing in the Louvre of Madame Destouche," writes M. Momméja, "is perhaps the most beautiful, the most worthy of being placed first in the series of those incomparable portraits which Ingres' pencil has rendered as immortal on their frail sheets of paper as are those that have been cut into indestructible bronze by the Italian medalists.

"Count Delaborde was, I believe, the first to remark upon this exquisite work. Writing of Ingres' drawings exhibited at the Salon des Arts-Unis in 1861, he says: 'The pencil portrait of Madame Destouche should especially be noticed – a drawing so masterly in its freedom, so fine in its picturesque quality, and in the originality of its costume.' And ten years later he wrote: 'This portrait is one of the most beautiful that Ingres ever drew.'

"Who then was this young woman who smiles so sweetly and takes such evident delight in her life and in her beauty? Possibly she was the wife of the artist Destouche, whose name figures on the list of David's pupils. Born in 1794, he must have married very young for Ingres to have drawn in Rome in 1816 a portrait of his wife, and yet the age of the lady here represented is quite suitable to that of a husband of twenty-two. Whoever she was, let us be grateful to her for having furnished Ingres with the subject for a masterpiece.

"She is truly elegant – Madame Destouche; her long gown, with its girdle just beneath the bust, is profusely trimmed with lace at the wrists and about the low-cut neck. A bit of delicate muslin, also edged with lace, covers her shoulders, and around her throat is a sort of ruff of plaited gauze, open in front to show the throat, around which is wound in a triple coil a chain with cross attached. As to her hat – it is a poem; a little peculiar, it may be, but charmingly becoming with its brim coquettishly turned up and with its high crown rounded like a cap beneath a cluster of nodding plumes....

"Never, perhaps, was the artist's delicate pencil more seductive, never did it more perfectly realize that physical charm of modeling which is like a caress, characteristic – as M. Roger Marx has truly said – of the creations of Ingres."

'THE STAMATY FAMILY' (DRAWING)

The family group reproduced in plate V, and now in the Bonnat Collection at Bayonne, is one of the finest examples of Ingres' work in pencil. It was drawn in Rome in 1818, and represents Monsieur Stamaty, consul at Città Vecchia, with his wife and children. "The characterization," writes M. Galichon, "is delicately and accurately given. Each person bears the stamp of his or her own individuality and is strikingly true to life. In short,

Ingres has here produced a masterpiece."

"A marvelous group," writes M. Lapauze, "in which the depth and intimacy of the feeling expressed is in no way marred by the wonderfully minute rendering of the accessories. Each little detail of costume, each fold of material, all the differences in texture – everything is given its own special character; everything is perceptible, tangible, so to speak. Science of draftsmanship, eloquence of line, could not possibly be carried farther."

'LA SOURCE'

'La Source' – The Spring – considered by Charles Blanc the most beautiful figure ever produced by the French school – was not painted until Ingres was seventy-six, though the study for it had been made many years before. In the admirable purity of its line, in its grace of form and its masterly modeling in light, this work has the beauty of a Greek statue.

Standing against a dark wall of rock, her little feet reflected in the pool of water at its base, is the nude figure of a young girl. One rounded arm is thrown above her head to help support against her shoulder a Grecian urn from which a stream of water falls into the pool beneath. With her blond hair, her smooth brow and clear blue eyes, her lips parted in a slight smile, her childish form, and her expression of unconsciousness and innocence, she is a figure of almost ideal loveliness.

Upon its completion 'La Source' was exhibited in Paris, and later in London. Everywhere it aroused feelings of enthusiastic admiration. The hypercritical, to be sure, found fault with the drawing of the legs, which, repainted by the artist when the picture was finished and the model no longer before him, are not carried so far as is the upper part of the body. But on the whole even those who most strenuously opposed Ingres' methods acknowledged its beauty and excellence.

"It is difficult to imagine," writes Mr. George Moore, "what further beauty he may have introduced into a face, or what further word he might have had to say on the beauty of a virgin body."

The picture was bought by Count Duchâtel, whose widow bequeathed it to the Louvre, where it now hangs. It is on canvas and measures five and a half feet high by two feet eight inches wide.

'PORTRAIT OF MONSIEUR BERTIN'

This celebrated portrait of Bertin, manager of the *Journal des Débats*, one of the leading papers of Paris, is generally regarded as the artist's masterpiece in portraiture. It was painted in 1832. Ingres has himself related how he made repeated studies for this work, frequently changing his original plan, and as frequently beginning over again; how anxious and discouraged he became; how he finally confessed to Monsieur Bertin that all the sittings had been in vain, that nothing had been accomplished, and how grateful he was when the busy man of affairs begged him not to be so distressed but to try once more, for that he, Bertin, was in no way weary, but would gladly give him as many sittings as he wished. Reassured by such consideration, Ingres took heart and resolved to make another attempt. The pose, however, perplexed him. While still undecided on this point it happened that he spent an evening in Bertin's house, and while there the conversation turned upon some political question of the day in which opposite views were held by Bertin and his sons. Each side vehemently maintained its ground, but no argument could convince the elder Bertin that the young men had reason on their side. While listening to their argument he leaned slightly forward in his armchair, and planting his hands squarely upon his knees turned toward the speaker with an expression on his strong face indicative of interest, lack of conviction, and consciousness of power to refute the argument advanced. The pose and expression – both so characteristic and unstudied – at once struck Ingres, and when he bade his host good night, "Monsieur Bertin," he said, "your portrait is done. I have you this time and shall not let you go."

The result, attained quickly and without effort, was the superb portrait here reproduced, so forceful and expressive, so true to life, that as we stand before it in the Louvre, where it now hangs, we seem to be in the presence of the man himself.

'THE VOW OF LOUIS XIII'

This great canvas, ordered by the Administration of the Fine Arts for the Cathedral of Montauban, where it is now to be seen in the sacristy, was begun in Florence in 1821, and finished three years later. The subject represents Louis xiii., King of France, consecrating to the Virgin his person, his crown, and his state, in recognition of the great mercy about to be vouchsafed by heaven in granting him an heir to his kingdom.

It would seem from his letters written at this period that Ingres was not altogether pleased with the "double subject" prescribed for him, and that, preferring one in which the interest should be more centered, he expressed his desire to paint instead 'The Assumption.' The Administration, however, was firm, and the artist was forced to yield. In his rendering of the scene, in which the historic and the mystical are combined, he has closely followed Raphael, taking his motives from that painter's famous pictures of 'The Transfiguration,' 'The Sistine Madonna,' 'The Madonna of Foligno,' and 'The Mass of Bolsena' (see Masters in Art, Vols. 1 and 4, Parts 12 and 40).

"Notwithstanding its manifest faults," writes M. Momméja, "this work is truly grand. It marks a turning-point in the history of painting as well as in the career of the artist whose fame it established. At the same time it was the beginning of his adherence to the academic method, which until then he had combated with such bitter violence.

"Exhibited at the Salon of 1824, 'The Vow of Louis XIII.' was received with unanimous approval. The romanticists, with Delacroix at their head, recognized in this new master the successful opponent of the teachings of David; while the classicists discovered in his conscientious drawing, sober and restrained coloring, an intentional protest against the innovators."

'PORTRAIT OF MADAME DEVAUÇAY'

In 1807, the year after his arrival in Rome, Ingres painted this portrait of Madame Devauçay, now in the Condé Museum, Chantilly, which for its purity of line, delicate subtlety of expression, and for its quality of distinction, ranks as one of his best and most characteristic works. The colors, too, partly owing, no doubt, to the mellowing effect of time, are richer and there is more atmosphere than in many of his paintings.

Madame Devauçay is seated in an armchair of red damask against a dark background. She wears a black velvet dress and a yellowish coffee-colored shawl. Around her throat is a necklace of brownish-red beads, and in one hand she holds a small tortoise-shell fan. Her smooth black hair is ornamented with a gold comb just visible at the back of her well-shaped head. Her eyes are dark, her complexion sallow, her features delicate, and although her face is in repose, about her mouth there lurks an inscrutable smile.

"Something in this canvas holds one captive," writes M. Lapauze, "even before one has had time to fully take in the perfection of the lines, the beauty of the arrangement, the velvety quality of the color. She is sister to Leonardo's 'Mona Lisa,' this woman of whom we cannot tell whether or not she is fair to look upon, so strongly does she appeal to our emotions.... She is as mysterious as the enigmatic creations of a Leonardo, or a Holbein, or as some of those beings portrayed by certain of the Primitives who have fixed upon their canvases the inexpressible emotions of the soul. Ingres, worshiper of form, consummate master of line, has here attained this rare power of magic."

'THE APOTHEOSIS OF HOMER'

In 1826, after his return from his first sojourn in Italy, Ingres was commissioned by the French government to decorate the ceiling of one of the galleries of the Louvre. For his subject the artist took 'The Apotheosis of Homer,' and in his treatment of the theme achieved what is regarded as his finest work in composition of the grand style.

Before the entrance to an Ionic temple, Homer, the blind Greek poet, is seated, like Jupiter, scepter in hand, upon a gilded throne. A winged figure of Victory, clad in rose-color, crowns him with a wreath of laurel, and on either side are grouped the most illustrious artists, poets, and musicians of all time. Here is Apelles leading Raphael by the hand; Æschylus presenting a scroll on which his tragedies are written; Phidias with his mallet; Pindar holding his lyre; Plato, Socrates, Horace, Virgil, and Dante, and, farther down, Shakespeare, Tasso, Corneille, Poussin, Gluck, Mozart, Racine, Molière, Fénelon, and others, while on the steps at Homer's feet, personified as the poet's daughters, are seated the 'Iliad' and the 'Odyssey.' The first is at the left, clad in red, and with Achilles' sword beside her; the other, enveloped in a sea-green mantle, is shown in profile, holding across her knee the oar of Ulysses.

In the loftiness of its style and the purity of its lines, 'The Apotheosis of Homer' is one of the noblest examples of the classic school of painting. Although it cannot be called in any way a copy of Raphael, it is evident that in painting it Ingres had in mind the 'Parnassus' and the 'School of Athens' (see Masters in Art, Vol. 4, Part 40), those grand creations of the painter whom he regarded as superior to all others.

A copy by his pupils now occupies the place of Ingres' great ceiling decoration. The original picture is exhibited in one of the rooms of the Louvre, where it is seen to better advantage. The figures are life-sized, and the canvas measures more than twelve feet high by nearly seventeen feet wide.

A LIST OF THE PRINCIPAL PAINTINGS BY INGRES WITH THEIR PRESENT LOCATIONS

BELGIUM. Brussels, Museum: Virgil reading the Æneid (study) – Liège, Museum: Napoleon Bonaparte as First Consul – ENGLAND. London, South Kensington Museum, Ionides Collection: Henry iv. and the Spanish Ambassador; Sleeping Odalisque – FRANCE. Aix, Museum: Jupiter and Thetis; Portrait of the Painter Granet – Angers, Museum: Francesca da Rimini – Autun, Cathedral: The Martyrdom of St. Symphorien – Chantilly, Condé Museum: Portrait of Madame Devauçay (Plate ix); Portrait of Ingres; Stratonice; Francesca da Rimini; Venus Anadyomene – Dampierre, Château of the Duke of Luynes: The Iron Age and The Golden Age (two unfinished mural paintings) – Montauban, Museum: Jesus among the Doctors; Ossian's Dream; Portrait of Ingres' Father; Portrait of Belvèze; Portrait of a Man – Montauban, Cathedral: The Vow of Louis xiii. (Plate viii) – Montpellier, Museum: Portrait of Desdebans; Stratonice; Oil Studies for 'Jesus among the Doctors; and 'The Apotheosis of Homer' – Nantes, Museum: Portrait of Madame de Senonnes (Plate ii) – Paris, Louvre: Christ giving the Keys of Heaven to St. Peter; The Apotheosis of Homer (Plate x); Œdipus and the Sphinx (Plate i);

'La Source' (Plate vi); The Virgin of the Host; Jeanne d'Arc at the Coronation of Charles vii.; Roger liberating Angelica; The Large Odalisque; The Bather; Portrait of M. Bertin (Plate vii); Portrait of Cherubini; Portrait of M. Cordier; Portraits of M. and Mme. Rivière; Portrait of Mlle. Rivière; Portrait of M. Bochet – Paris, École des Beaux-arts: Romulus victorious over Acron, King of the Sabines; The Ambassadors of Agamemnon in the Tent of Achilles – Paris, Hôtel des Invalides: Portrait of Napoleon Bonaparte – Paris, Théatre Français: Louis xiv. and Molière – Paris, Collection Of M. Degas: Portraits of M. and Mme. Leblanc – Perpignan, Museum: Portrait of the Duke of Orleans (repetition of the one at Versailles) – Rouen, Museum: 'La belle Zélie' – Toulouse, Museum: Virgil reading the Æneid – Versailles, Palace: Portrait of the Duke of Orleans – ITALY, Florence, Uffizi Gallery: Portrait of Ingres (see page 274) – Rome, Quirinal Palace: Ossian's Dream – Rome, Villa Miollis: Virgil reading the Æneid – RUSSIA, St. Petersburg, Imperial Collections: The Virgin of the Host – SWITZERLAND. Coppet, Château: Portrait of the Comtesse d'Haussonville.

INGRES BIBLIOGRAPHY

A LIST OF THE PRINCIPAL BOOKS AND MAGAZINE
ARTICLES DEALING WITH INGRES

Alexandre, A. Jean-Dominique Ingres, Master of Pure Draughtsmanship. London, 1905 – Alexandre, A. Histoire populaire de la peinture; école française. Paris [1893] – Amaury-Duval. L'Atelier d'Ingres. Paris, 1878 – Balze, R. Ingres: son école, son enseignement du dessin. Paris, 1880 – Beulé, C. E. Éloge de M. Ingres. Paris, 1867 – Blanc, C. Ingres, sa vie et ses ouvrages. Paris, 1870 – Brownell, W. C. French Art. New York, 1901 – Chennevières, H. de. Les dessins du Louvre. Paris, 1882-83 – Chesneau, E. La peinture française au XIXe siècle. Paris, 1862 – Chesneau, E. Peintres et statuaires romantiques. Paris, 1880 – Cook, C. Art and Artists of Our Time. New York, 1888 – Delaborde, H. Ingres, sa vie, ses travaux, sa doctrine. Paris, 1870 – Delécluze, E. J. David, son école et son temps. Paris, 1855 – Duplessis, G. Les portraits dessinés par Ingres. Paris, 1896 – Forestié, E. Notice sur le monument d'Ingres érigé à Montauban. Montauban, 1871 – Gautier, T. Portraits contemporains. Paris, 1881 – Gigoux, J. Causeries sur les artistes de mon temps. Paris, 1885 – Gonse, L. Les chefs-d'œuvre des Musées de France. Paris, 1900 – Grandmougin, C. Ingres (in La Grande Encyclopédie).

Paris, 1886-1902 – Gruyère, F.-A. La peinture au château de Chantilly. Paris, 1898 – Haack, Dr. F. Die Kunst XIX Jahrhunderts. Stuttgart, 1905 – Hamerton, P. G. Contemporary French Painters. London, 1868 – Kingsley, R. G. A History of French Art. London, 1899 – Lapauze, H. Mélanges sur l'art français. Paris, 1905 – Larroumet, G. Portrait de Bertin l'ainé (in Jouin's Chefs-d'œuvre). Paris, 1899 – Loménie, L. Galerie des contemporains illustres. Paris, 1842 – MacColl, D. S. Nineteenth Century Art. Glasgow, 1902 – Marcel, H. La peinture française au XIXe siècle. Paris [1906] – Mauclair, C. The Great French Painters. London, 1903 – Merson, O. Ingres, sa vie et ses œuvres. Paris, 1867 – Michel, A. Notes sur l'art moderne. Paris, 1896 – Momméja, J. Ingres. Paris [1903] – Montrosier, E. Peintres modernes. Paris, 1882 – Moore G. Modern Painting. New York, 1893 – Muther, R. The History of Modern Painting. London, 1895 – Muther, R. Ein Jahrhundert französischer Malerei. Berlin, 1901 – Pattison, E. F. S. Ingres (in Encyclopædia Britannica). Edinburgh, 1883 – Perrier, C. Études sur les beaux-arts en France et à l'étranger. Paris, 1863 – Pinset, R., and D'Auriac, J. Histoire du portrait en France. Paris, 1884 – Planche, J. B. G. Portraits d'artistes. Paris, 1853 – Planche, J. B. G. Études sur les arts. Paris, 1855 – Schmarsow, A. Jean-Auguste-Dominique Ingres (in Dohme's Kunst und Künstler, etc.) Leipsic, 1886 – Silvestre, T. Histoire des artistes vivants. Paris, 1856 – Silvestre, T. Les artistes français. Paris, 1878 – Silvestre, T. L'apothéose de M. Ingres. Paris, 1862 – Stranahan, C. H. A History of French Painting. New York, 1888 – Wyzewa, T. de, and Perreau, X. Les grands peintres de la France. Paris, 1890.

CONTEMPORARY REVIEW, 1867: T. F. Wedmore; Ingres –
Gazette Des Beaux-Arts, 1861: É. Galichon; Dessins de M. Ingres.
1861: H. Delaborde; Les dessins de M. Ingres. 1861: É. Galichon;
Description des dessins de M. Ingres exposés au Salon des Arts-
Unis. 1862: H. Delaborde; La collection de tableaux de M. le
comte Duchâtel. 1862: H. Delaborde; De quelques traditions de
l'art français. 1863: C. Blanc; Du style et de M. Ingres. 1867: É.
Galichon; La mort de M. Ingres. 1867-68: C. Blanc; Ingres, sa vie
et ses ouvrages. 1870: H. Delaborde; Notes et pensées de J.-A.-D.
Ingres. 1870: G. Duplessis; Le cabinet de M. Gatteaux. 1870: J. B.;
Deux historiens d'Ingres. 1889: P. Mantz; La peinture française.
1894: L. Mabilleau; Les dessins d'Ingres au Musée de Montauban.
1898: G. Babin; Madame de Senonnes par Ingres. 1898: La
jeunesse d'Ingres. 1900: A. Michel; La peinture française à
l'exposition centennale. 1901: E. Hébert; La Villa Medicis en 1840:
Souvenirs d'un pensionnaire. 1905: J. Momméja; Le portrait de
Madame Destouches – Die Kunst, 1901: H. von Tschudi; Die
Jahrhundert-Ausstellung der französischen Kunst – McClure's
Magazine, 1896: W. H. Low; A Century of Painting – MacMillan's
Magazine, 1871: F. Wedmore; Ingres – Revue de Paris, 1896: L.
Mabilleau; Les cahiers d'Ingres au Musée de Montauban –
Zeitschrift für Bildende Kunst, 1867: J. Meyer; Ingres.

Contemporaries of Ingres on the following pages.

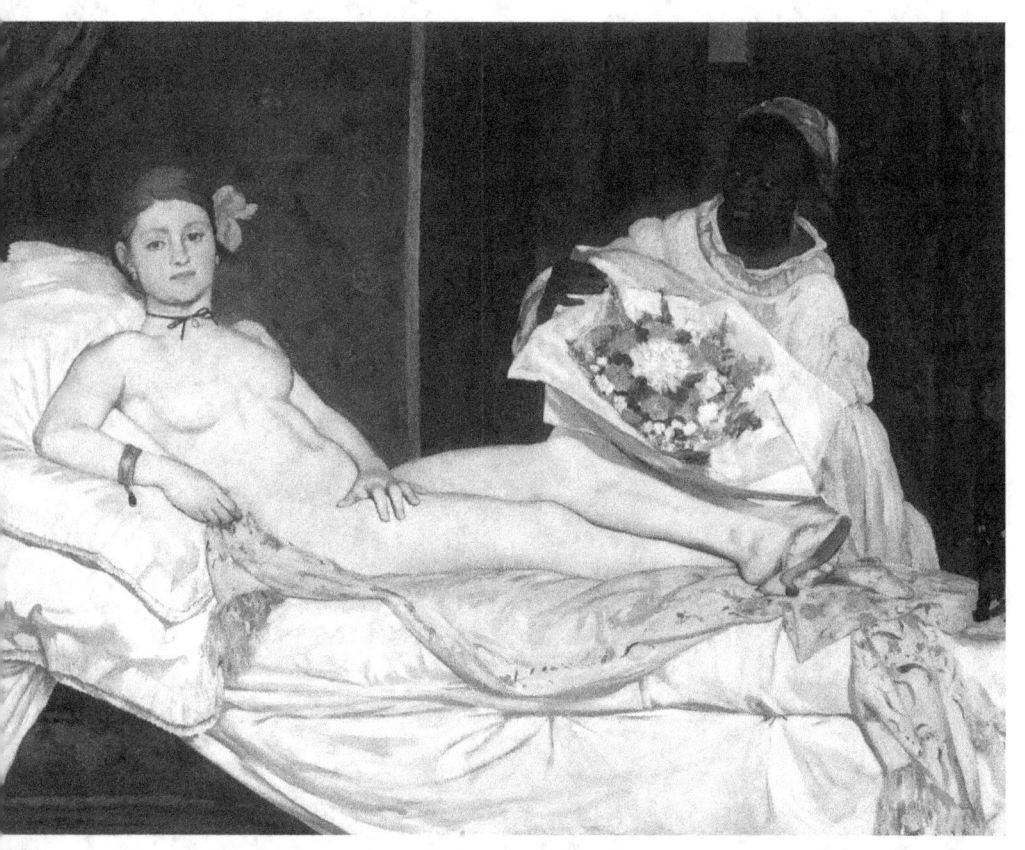

Edouard Manet, Olympia, Musée d'Orsay, Paris

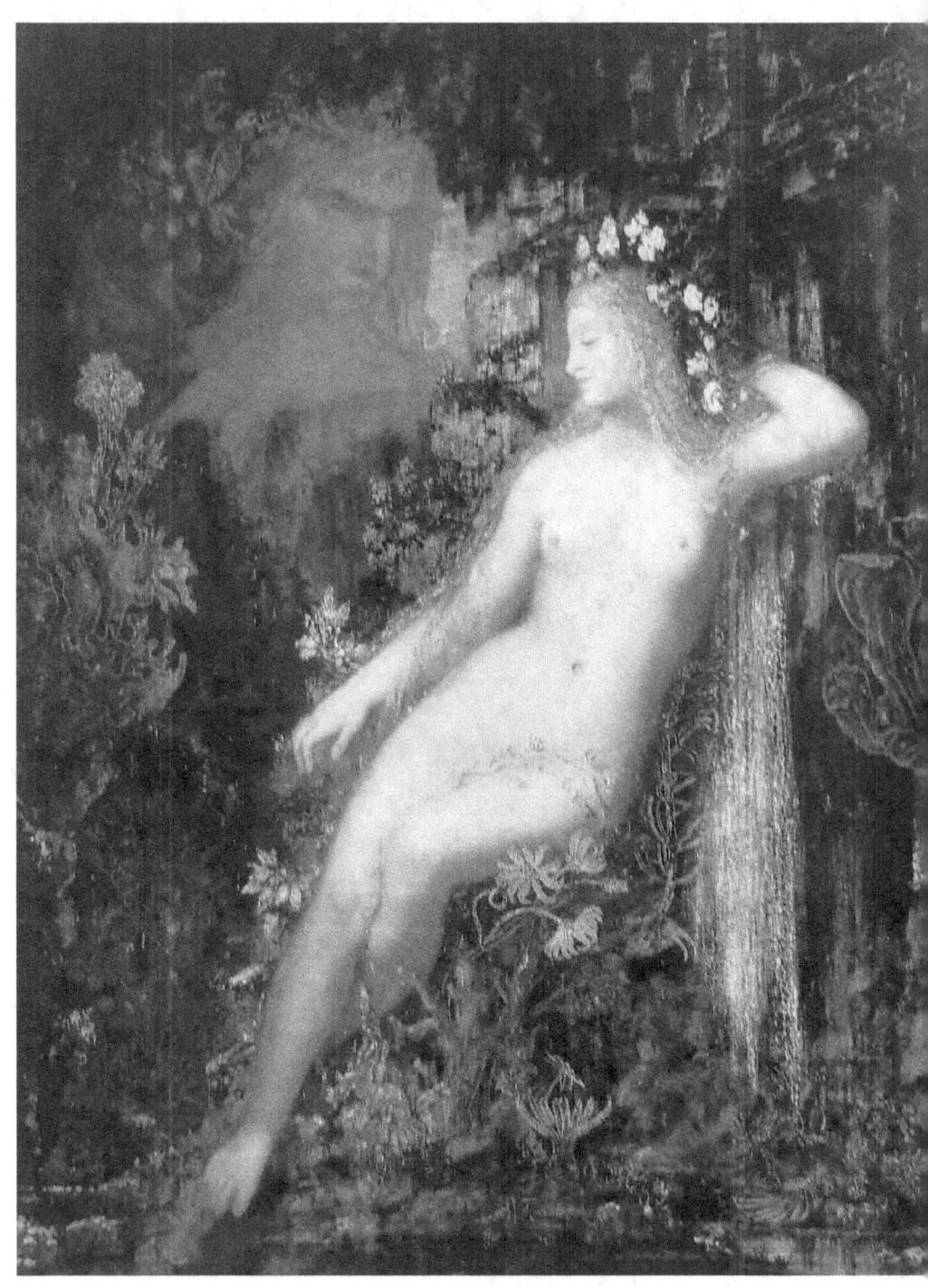

Gustave Moreau, Galatea, 1880

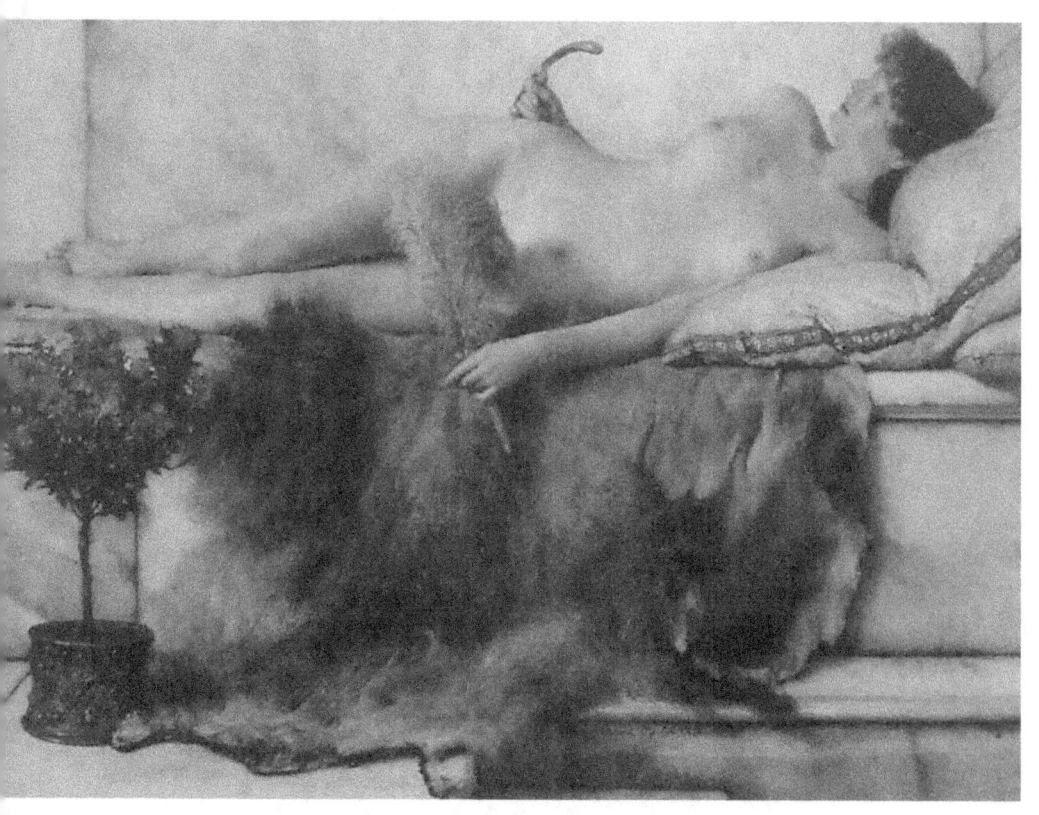

Lawrence Alma-Tadema, In the Tepidarium, 1881,
Lady Lever Art Gallery, Liverpool

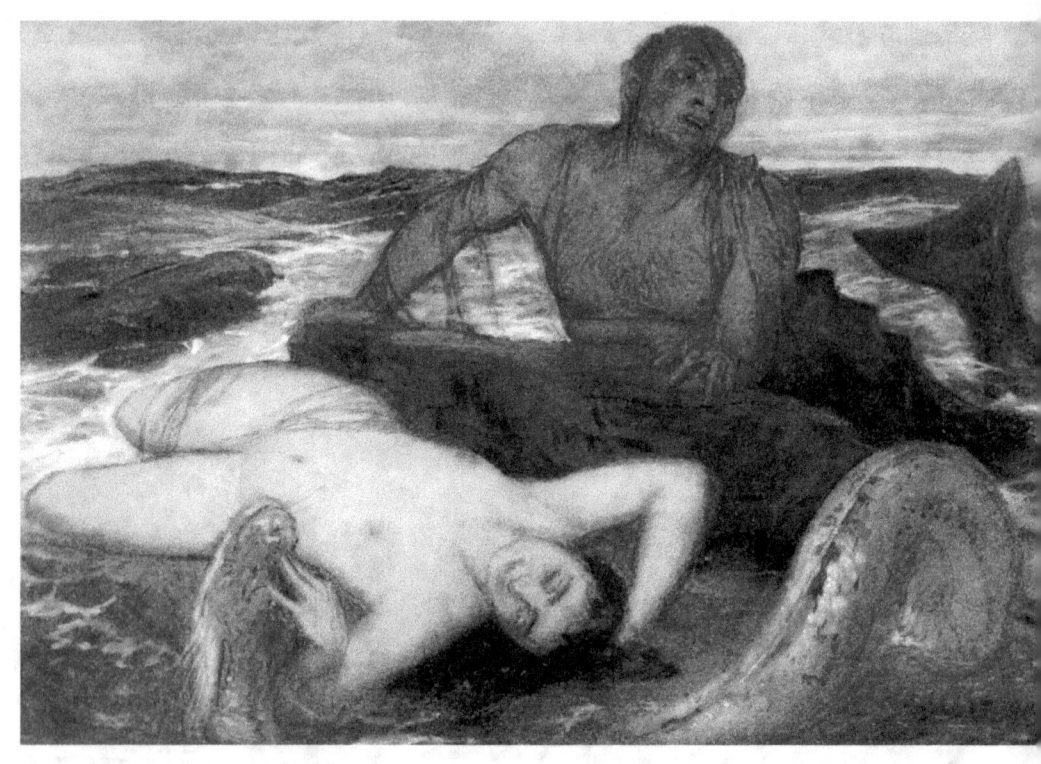

Arnold Böcklin, Triton and Nereid, 1877

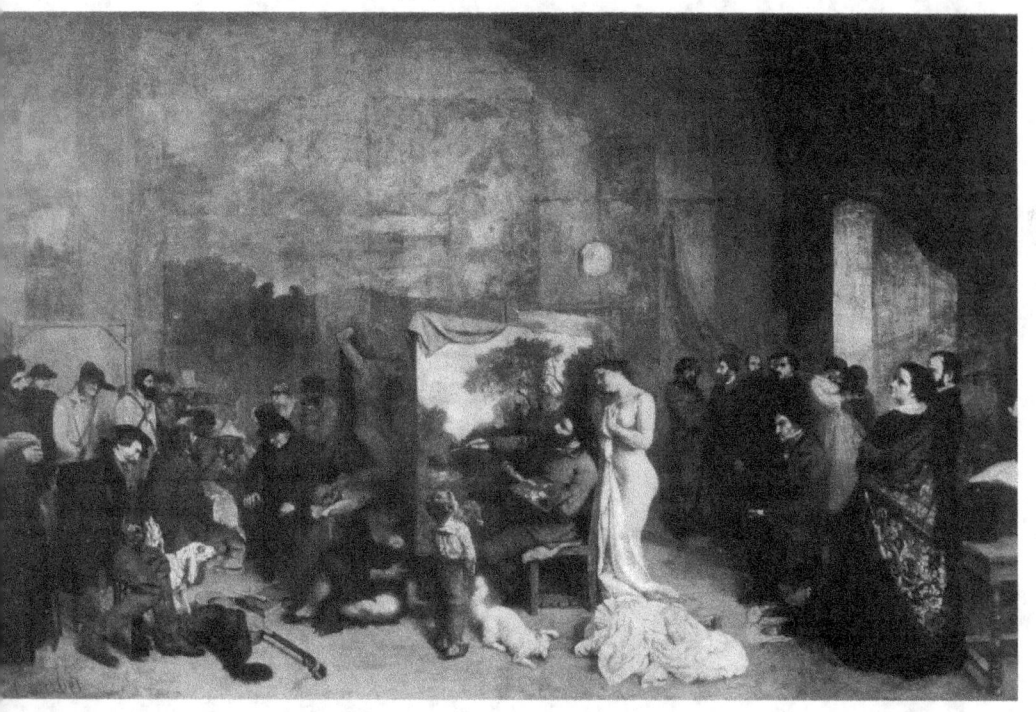

Gustave Courbet, The Studio, 1855, Musée d'Orsay, Paris

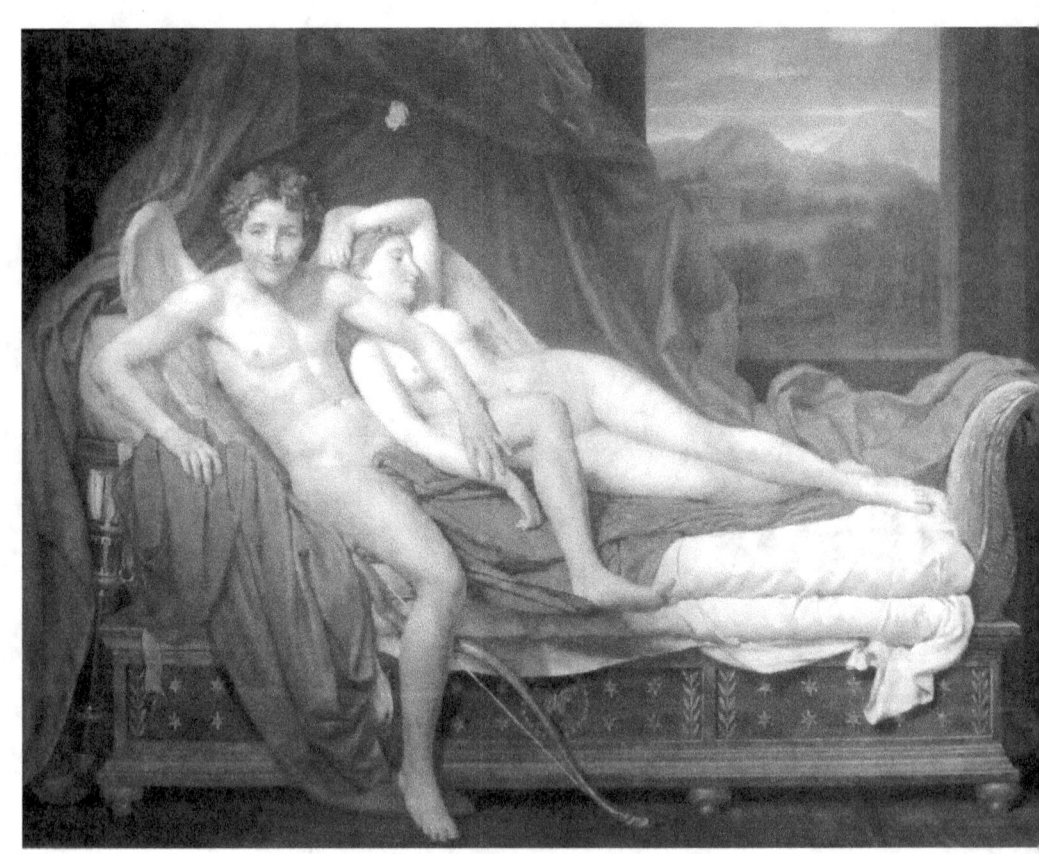

Jacques-Louis David, Cupid and Psyche, 1817,
Cleveland Museum of Art

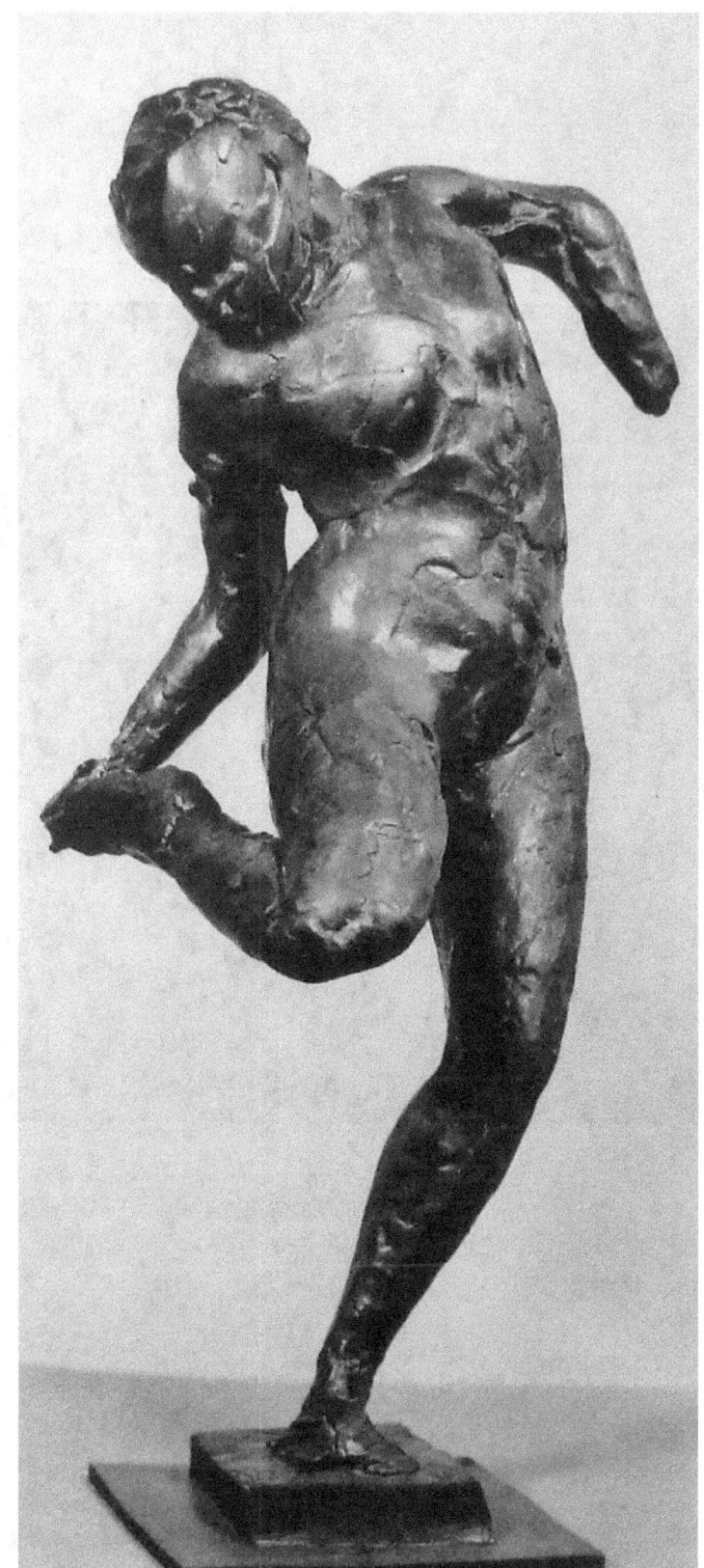

Edgar Degas,
Dancer Looking At
the Sole of Her
Right Foot, 1882-95,
New York

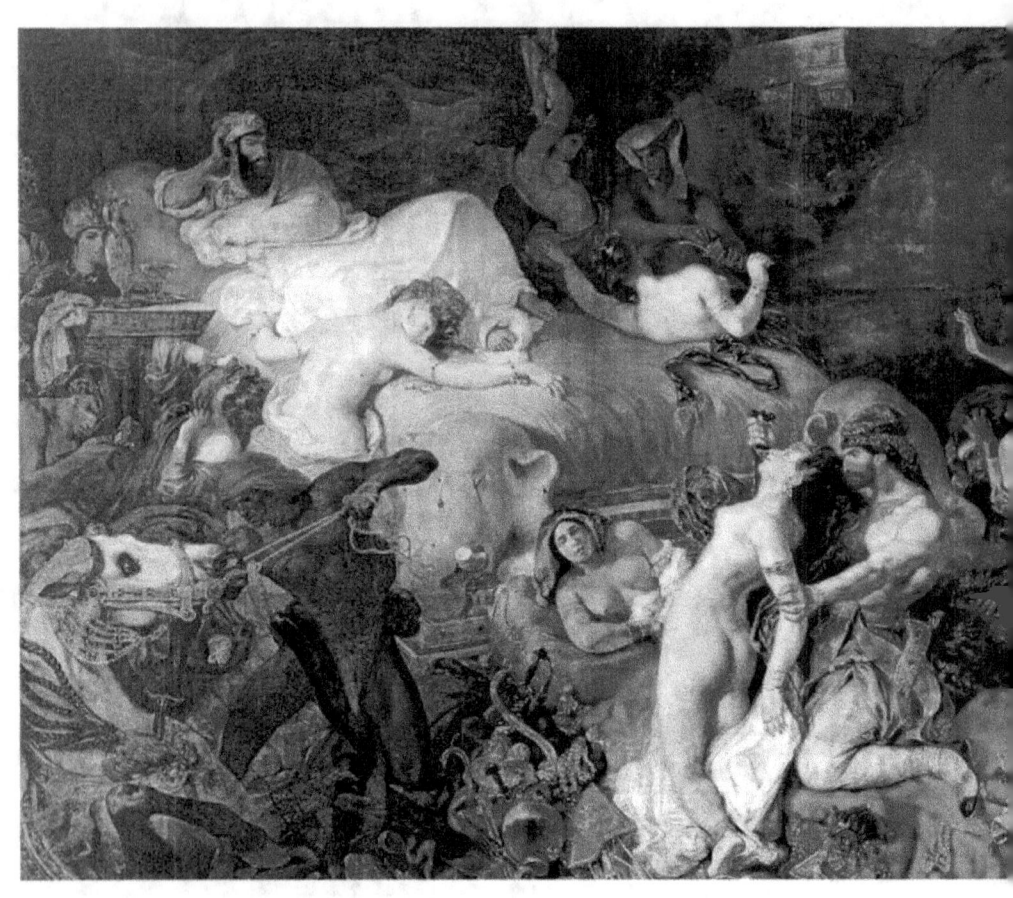

Eugène Delacroix, The Death of Sardanapalus, 1827
(this page and over).

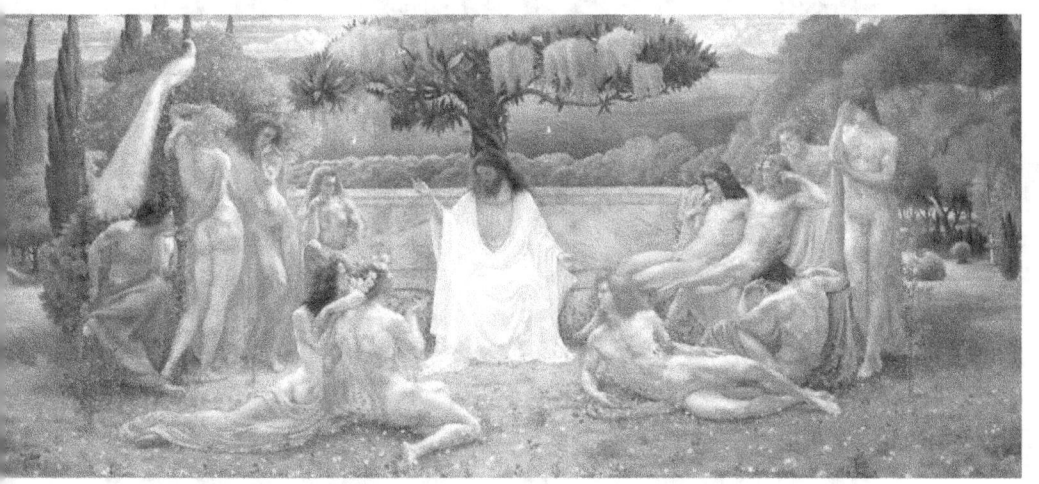

Jean Delville, The School of Plato, 1898

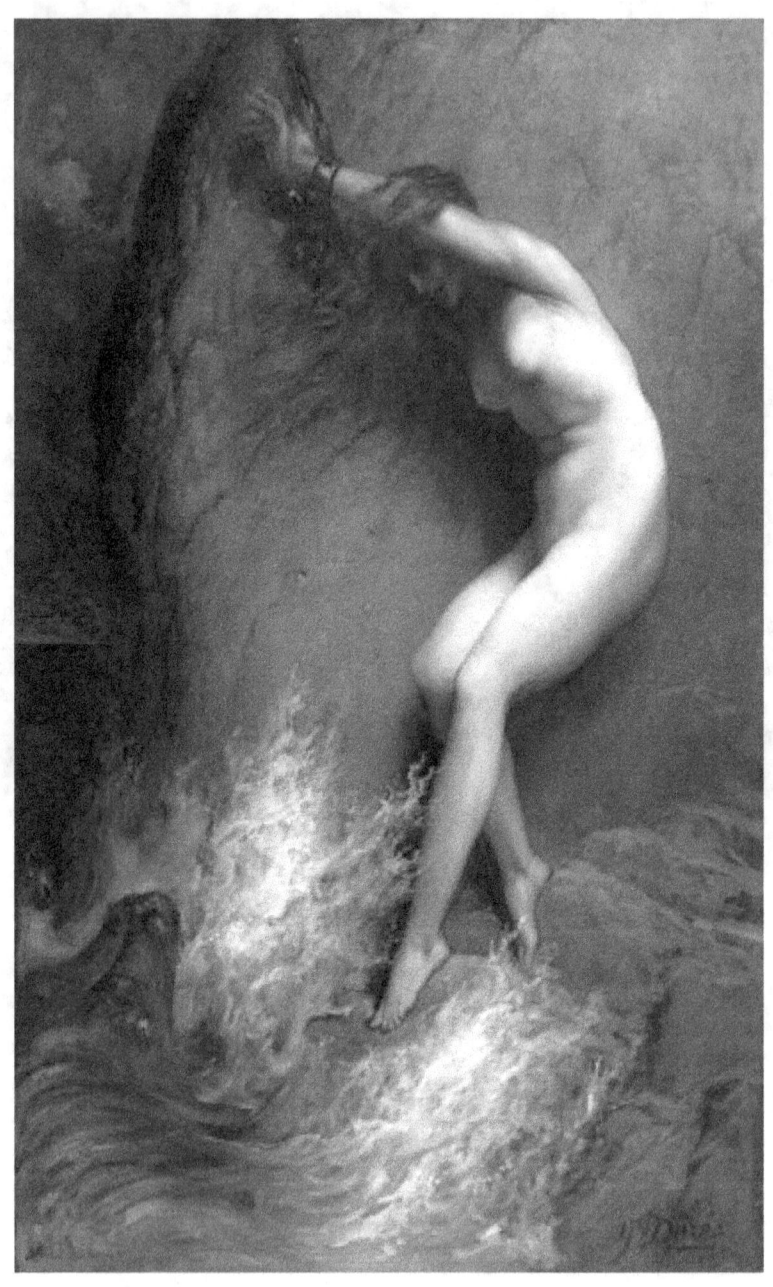

Gustave Doré

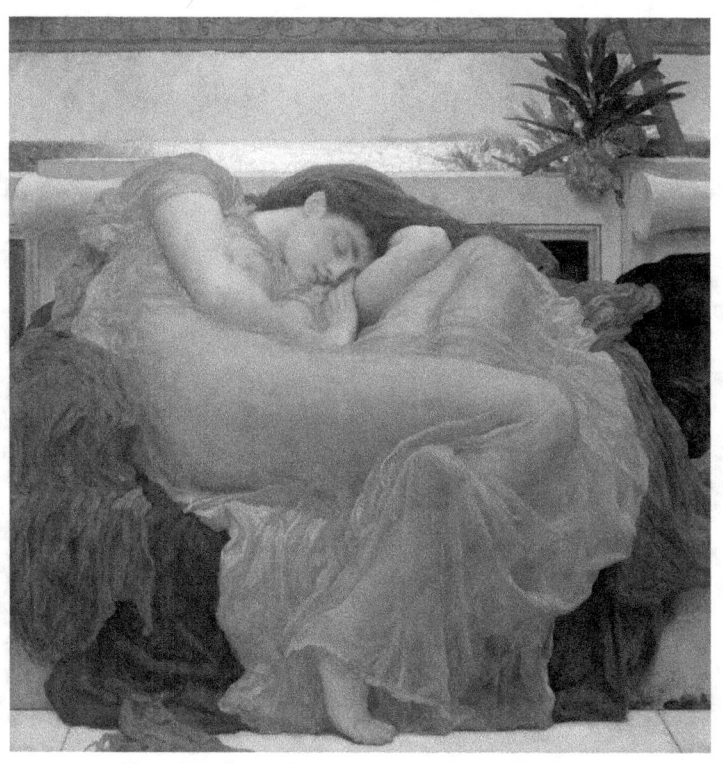

Lord Leighton, Flaming June, 1895, Puerto Rico

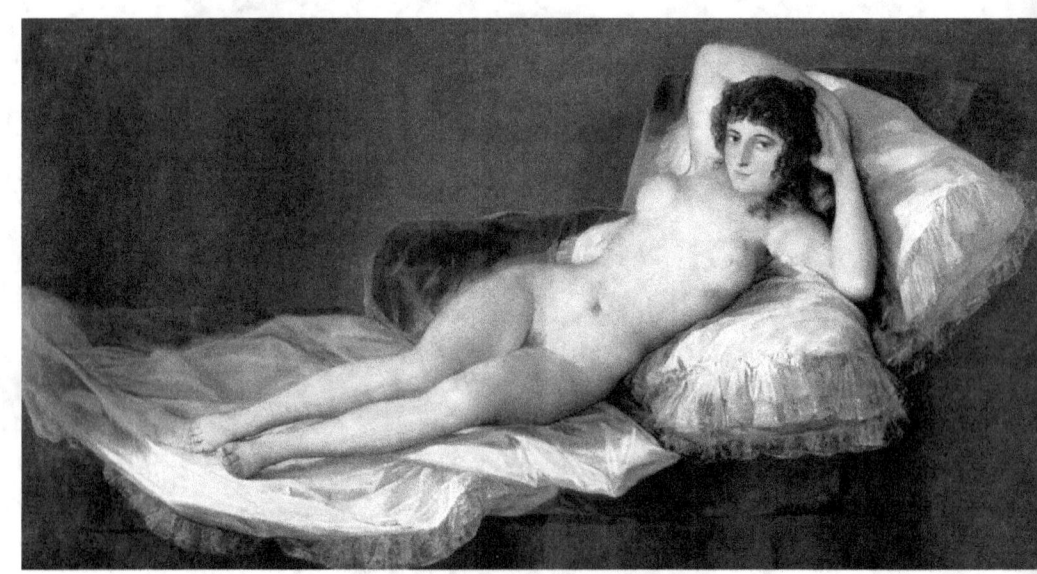

Francisco de Goya, Naked Maja, c. 1801, Prado, Madrid

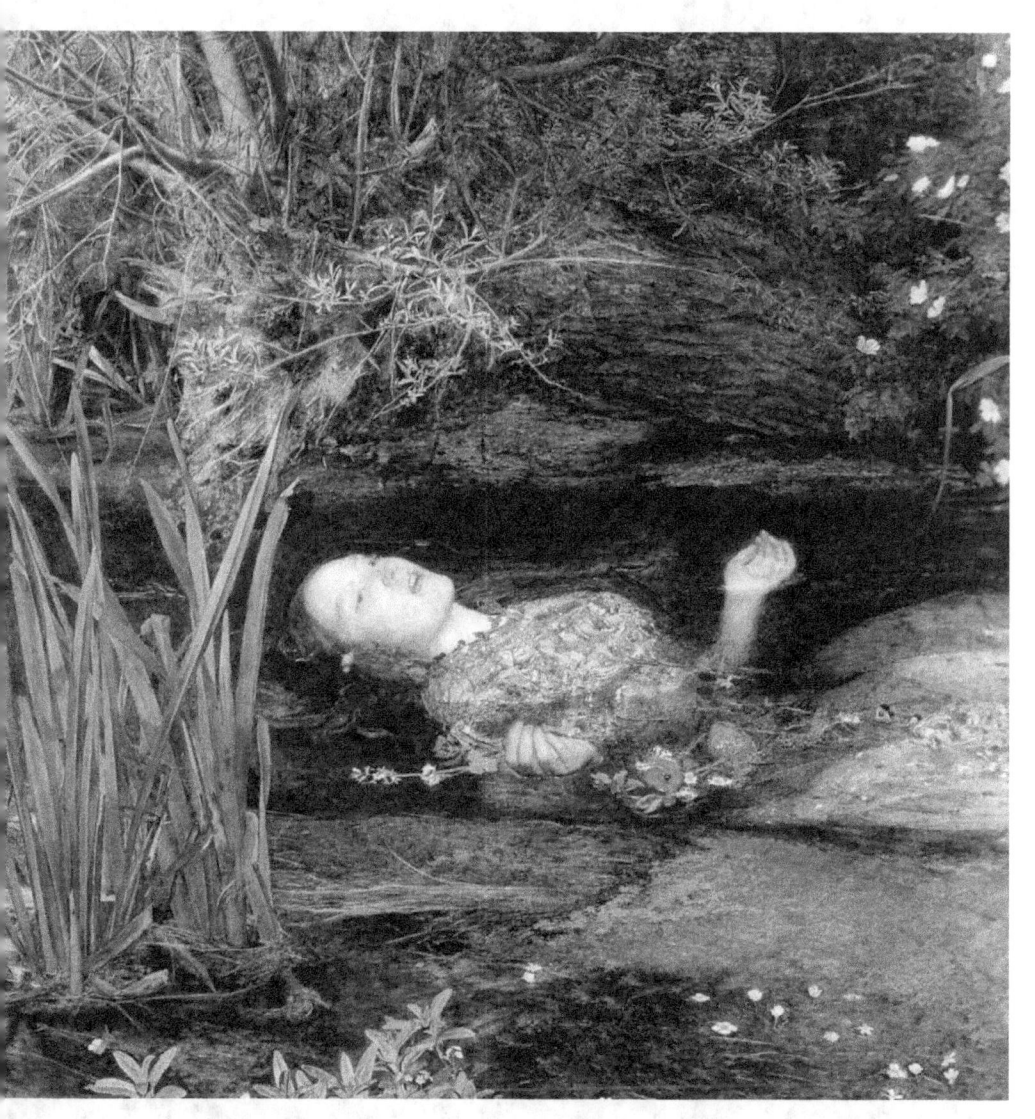

John Everett Millais, Ophelia.

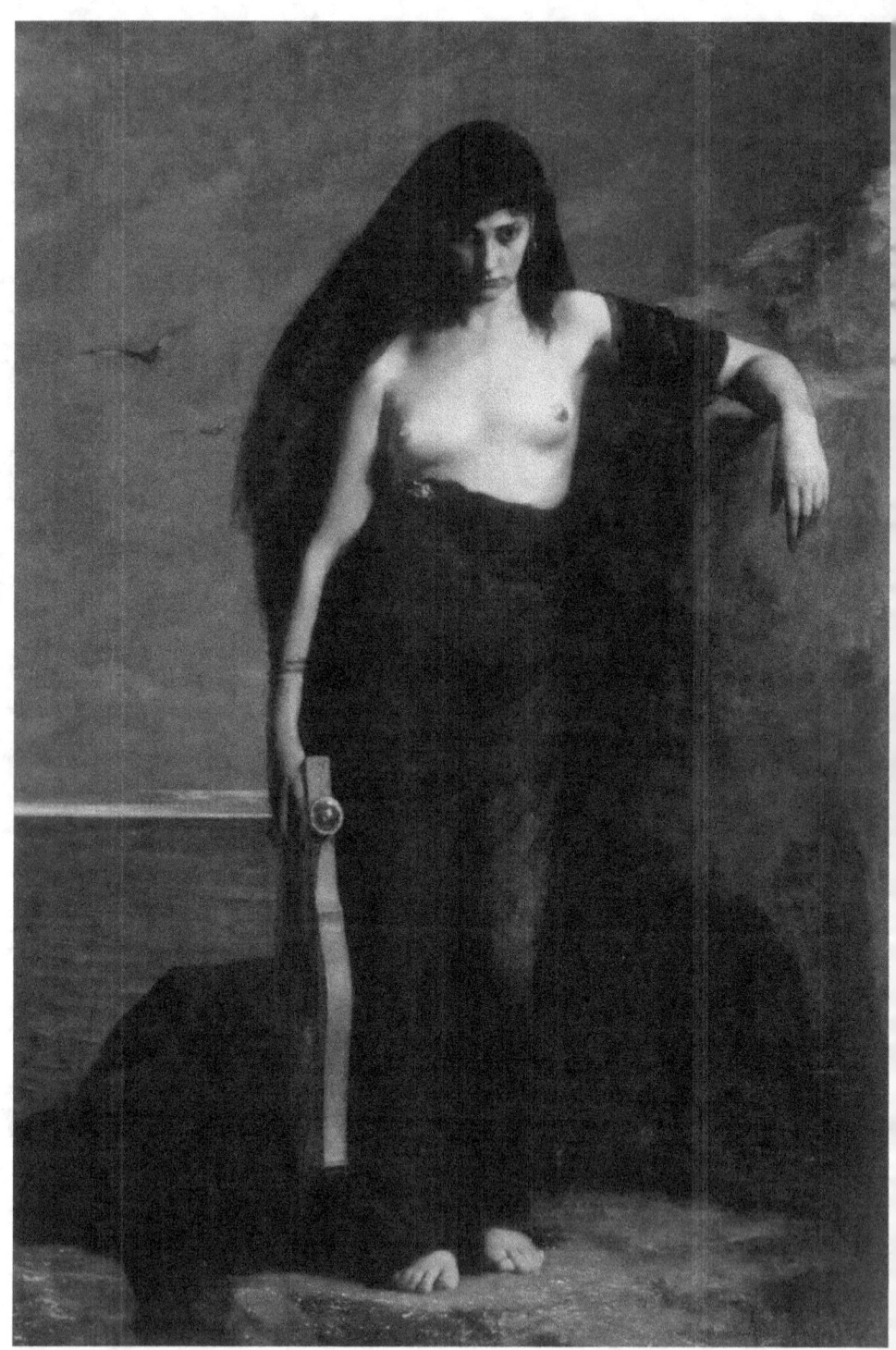

Charles Mengin, Sappho, 1867, Manchester

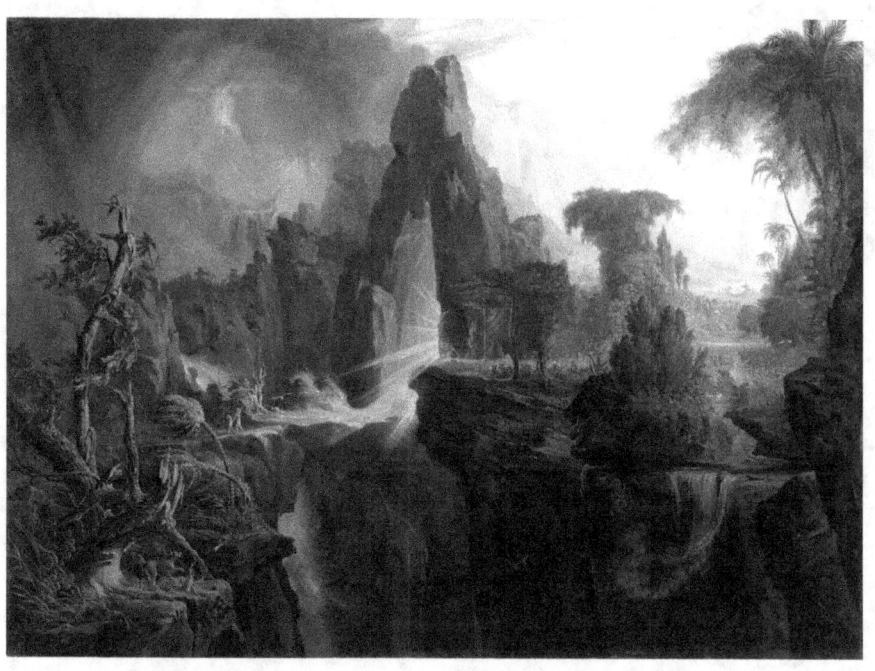

Thomas Cole, Expulsion From the Garden of Eden, 1828,
Museum of Fine Arts, Boston

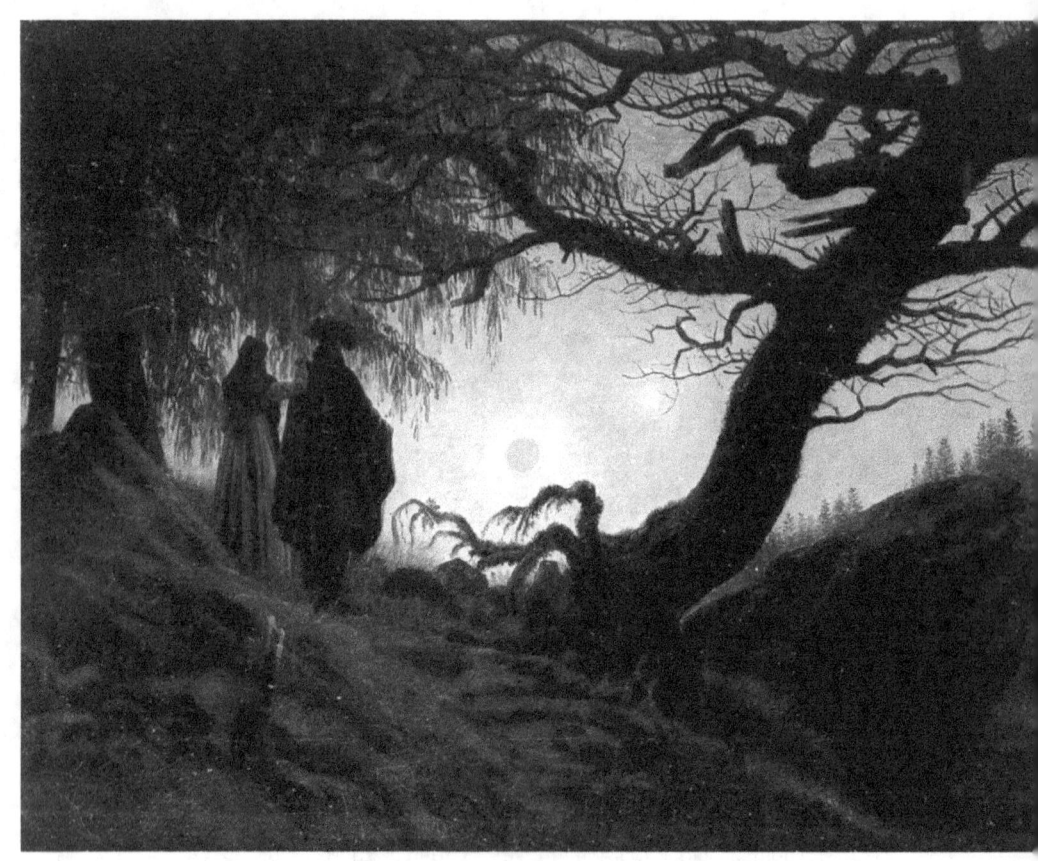

Caspar David Friedrich, Man and
Woman Contemplating the Moon,
1830-35, Alte Nationalgalerie

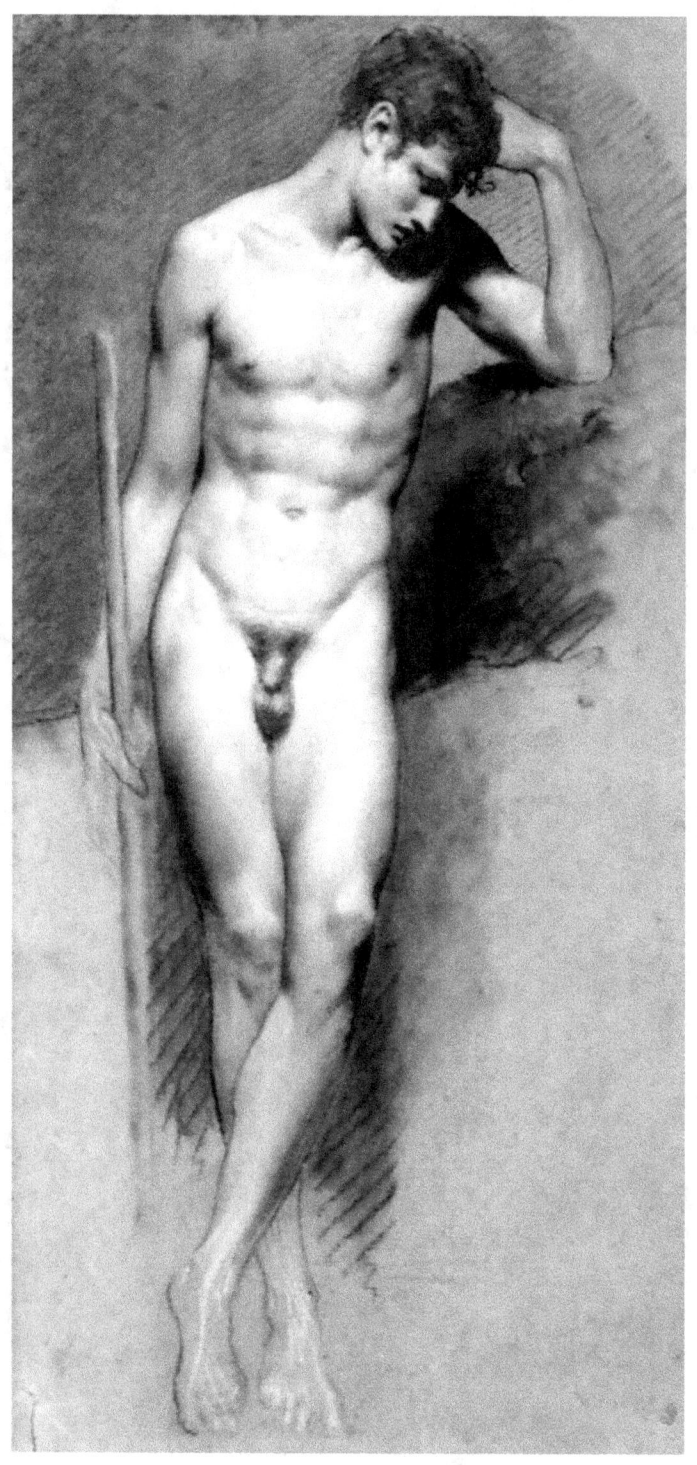

Pierre-Paul Prud'hon (1758-1823), Male Nude Standing

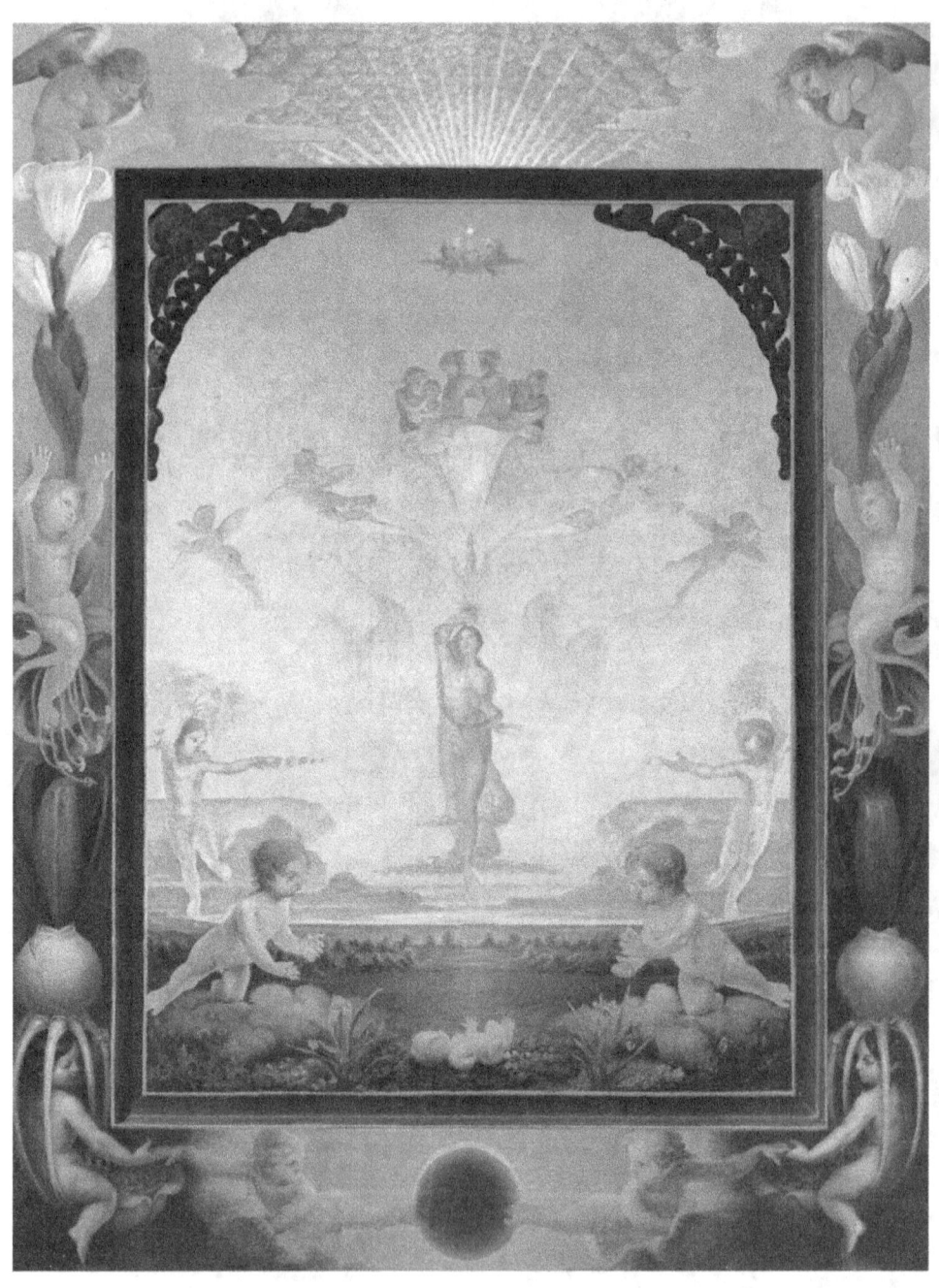

Philipp Otto Runge, Morning, 1808, Hamburg

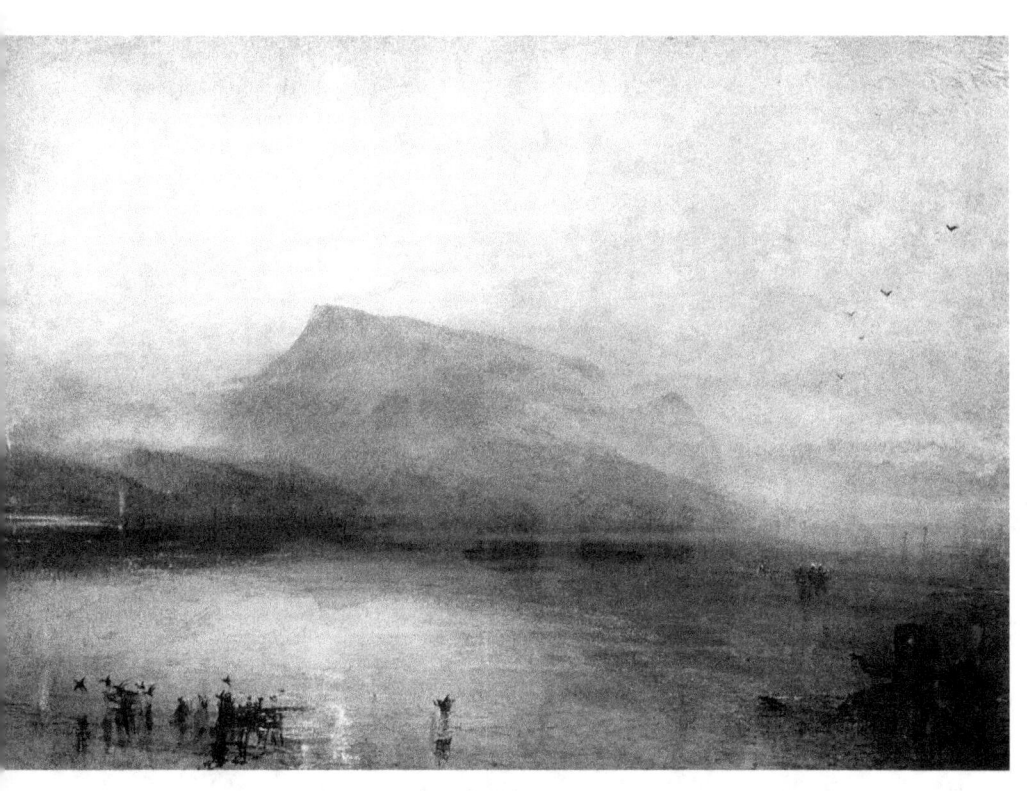

J.M.W. Turner, The Blue Rigi, Lake of Lucerne, Sunrise,
1842, Clore Gallery, London

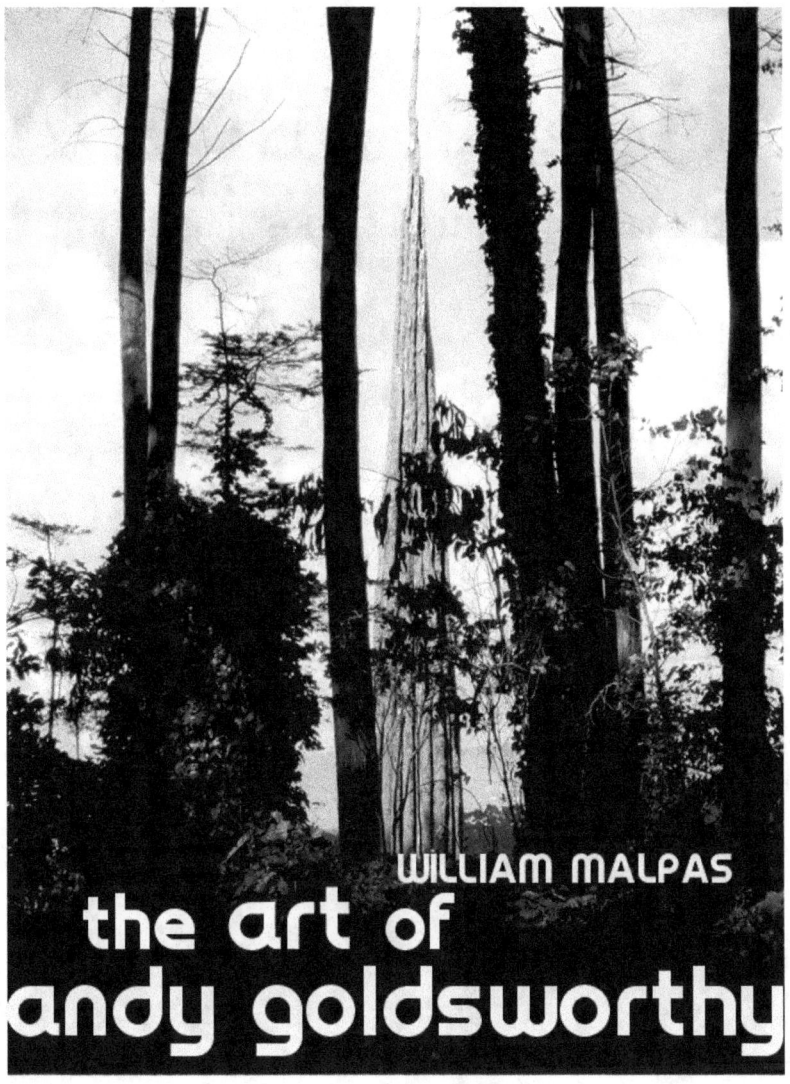

WILLIAM MALPAS
the art of
andy goldsworthy

This is the most comprehensive and detailed account of the art of Andy Goldsworthy available.

This study of Andy Goldsworthy discusses all of Goldsworthy's major exhibitions, books and projects, including the *Sheepfolds* project; *Garden of Stones* in New York; TV and dance collaborations; and the books *Wood, Stone, Time* and *Passage*. William Malpas surveys all of Goldsworthy's output, and analyzes his relation with other land artists such as Robert Smithson, the Christos, Walter de Maria, Chris Drury, Richard Long and David Nash; women sculptors; sculpture in the modern era; and Goldsworthy's place in the contemporary British art scene.

The book has been updated and revised for this new edition.

ISBN 9781861714107 Pbk   ISBN 9781861714114 Hbk
Fully illustrated   www.crmoon.com

MAURICE SENDAK

& the art of children's book illustration

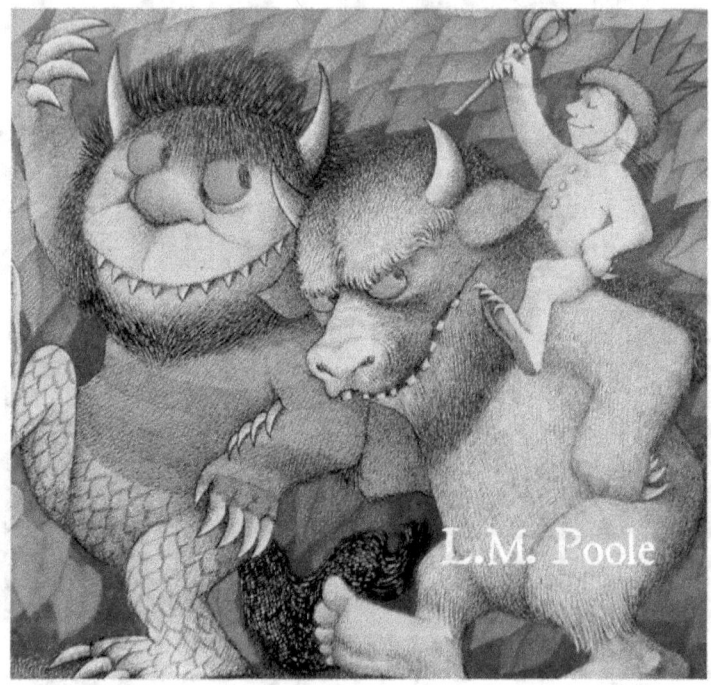

L.M. Poole

Maurice Sendak is the widely acclaimed American children's book author and illustrator. This critical study focuses on his famous trilogy, *Where the Wild Things Are*, *In the Night Kitchen* and *Outside Over There*, as well as the early works and Sendak's superb depictions of the Grimm Brothers' fairy tales in *The Juniper Tree*. L.M. Poole begins with a chapter on children's book illustration, in particular the treatment of fairy tales. Sendak's work is situated within the history of children's book illustration, and he is compared with many contemporary authors.

Fully illustrated. The book has been revised and updated for this edition.
ISBN 9781861714282 Pbk   ISBN 9781861713469 Hbk

Beauties, Beasts, and Enchantment

CLASSIC FRENCH FAIRY TALES

Translated and with an Introduction
by Jack Zipes

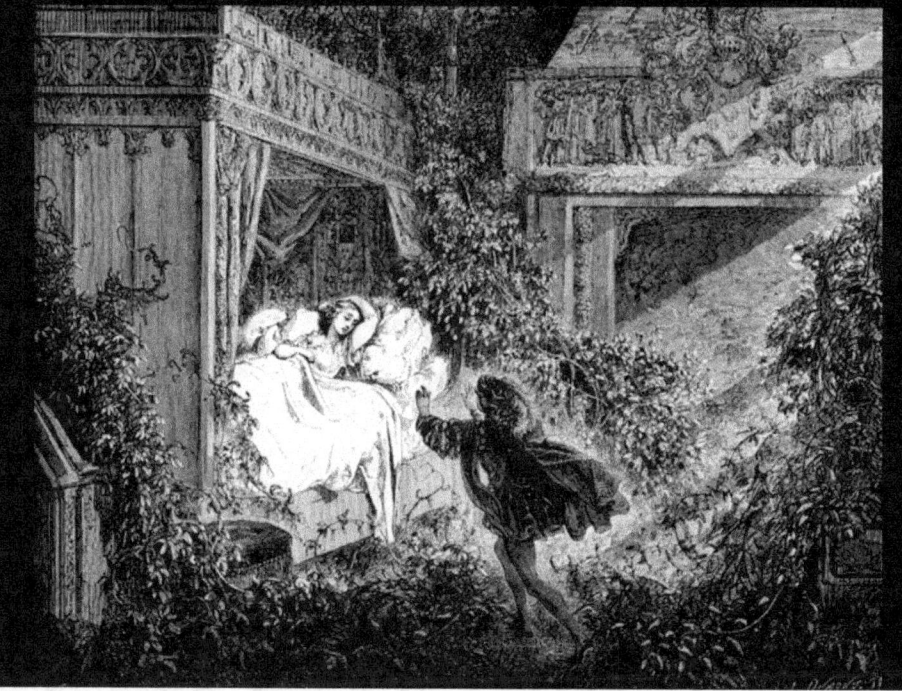

A collection of 36 classic French fairy tales translated by renowned writer Jack Zipes.
Cinderella, Beauty and the Beast, Sleeping Beauty and *Little Red Riding Hood* are among the
classic fairy tales in this amazing book.
Includes illustrations from fairy tale collections.
Jack Zipes has written and published widely on fairy tales.

'Terrific... a succulent array of 17th and 18th century 'salon' fairy tales'
- *The New York Times Book Review*

'These tales are adventurous, thrilling in a way fairy tales are meant to be... The translation
from the French is modern, happily free of archaic and hyperbolic language... a fine and
sophisticated collection' - *New York Tribune*

'Enjoyable to read... a unique collection of French regional folklore' - *Library Journal*

'Charming stories accompanied by attractive pen-and-ink drawings' - *Chattanooga Times*

Introduction and illustrations   612pp.   ISBN 9781861712510 Pbk   ISBN 9781861713193 Hbk

CRESCENT MOON PUBLISHING

web: www.crmoon.com e-mail: cresmopub@yahoo.co.uk

ARTS, PAINTING, SCULPTURE

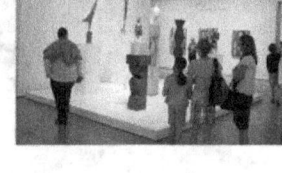
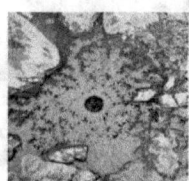
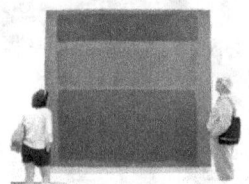

The Art of Andy Goldsworthy
Andy Goldsworthy: Touching Nature
Andy Goldsworthy in Close-Up
Andy Goldsworthy: Pocket Guide
Andy Goldsworthy In America
Land Art: A Complete Guide
The Art of Richard Long
Richard Long: Pocket Guide
Land Art In the UK
Land Art in Close-Up
Land Art In the U.S.A.
Land Art: Pocket Guide
Installation Art in Close-Up
Minimal Art and Artists In the 1960s and After
Colourfield Painting
Land Art DVD, TV documentary
Andy Goldsworthy DVD, TV documentary
The Erotic Object: Sexuality in Sculpture From Prehistory to the Present Day
Sex in Art: Pornography and Pleasure in Painting and Sculpture
Postwar Art
Sacred Gardens: The Garden in Myth, Religion and Art
Glorification: Religious Abstraction in Renaissance and 20th Century Art
Early Netherlandish Painting
Leonardo da Vinci
Piero della Francesca
Giovanni Bellini
Fra Angelico: Art and Religion in the Renaissance
Mark Rothko: The Art of Transcendence
Frank Stella: American Abstract Artist
Jasper Johns
Brice Marden
Alison Wilding: The Embrace of Sculpture
Vincent van Gogh: Visionary Landscapes
Eric Gill: Nuptials of God
Constantin Brancusi: Sculpting the Essence of Things
Max Beckmann
Caravaggio
Gustave Moreau
Egon Schiele: Sex and Death In Purple Stockings
Delizioso Fotografico Fervore: Works In Process I
Sacro Cuore: Works In Process 2
The Light Eternal: J.M.W. Turner
The Madonna Glorified: Karen Arthurs

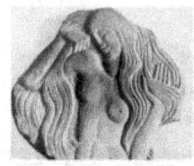
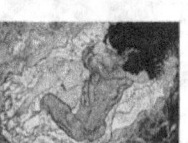
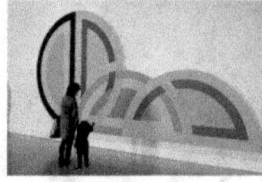
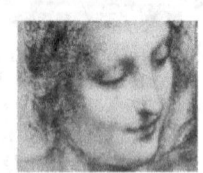
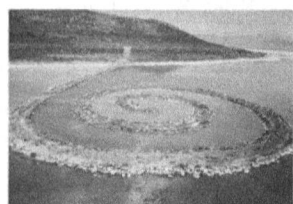

LITERATURE

J.R.R. Tolkien: The Books, The Films, The Whole Cultural Phenomenon
J.R.R. Tolkien: Pocket Guide
Tolkien's Heroic Quest
The *Earthsea* Books of Ursula Le Guin
Beauties, Beasts and Enchantment: Classic French Fairy Tales
German Popular Stories by the Brothers Grimm
Philip Pullman and *His Dark Materials*
Sexing Hardy: Thomas Hardy and Feminism
Thomas Hardy's *Tess of the d'Urbervilles*
Thomas Hardy's *Jude the Obscure*
Thomas Hardy: The Tragic Novels
Love and Tragedy: Thomas Hardy
The Poetry of Landscape in Hardy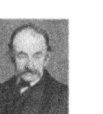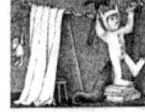
Wessex Revisited: Thomas Hardy and John Cowper Powys
Wolfgang Iser: Essays and Interviews
Petrarch, Dante and the Troubadours
Maurice Sendak and the Art of Children's Book Illustration
Andrea Dworkin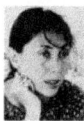
Cixous, Irigaray, Kristeva: The *Jouissance* of French Feminism
Julia Kristeva: Art, Love, Melancholy, Philosophy, Semiotics and Psychoanalysis
Hélene Cixous I Love You: The *Jouissance* of Writing
Luce Irigaray: Lips, Kissing, and the Politics of Sexual Difference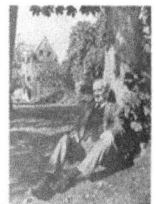
Peter Redgrove: Here Comes the Flood
Peter Redgrove: Sex-Magic-Poetry-Cornwall
Lawrence Durrell: Between Love and Death, East and West
Love, Culture & Poetry: Lawrence Durrell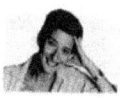
Cavafy: Anatomy of a Soul
German Romantic Poetry: Goethe, Novalis, Heine, Hölderlin
Feminism and Shakespeare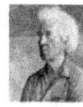
Shakespeare: Love, Poetry & Magic
The Passion of D.H. Lawrence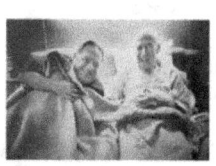
D.H. Lawrence: Symbolic Landscapes
D.H. Lawrence: Infinite Sensual Violence
Rimbaud: Arthur Rimbaud and the Magic of Poetry
The Ecstasies of John Cowper Powys
Sensualism and Mythology: The Wessex Novels of John Cowper Powys
Amorous Life: John Cowper Powys and the Manifestation of Affectivity (H.W. Fawkner)
Postmodern Powys: New Essays on John Cowper Powys (Joe Boulter)
Rethinking Powys: Critical Essays on John Cowper Powys
Paul Bowles & Bernardo Bertolucci
Rainer Maria Rilke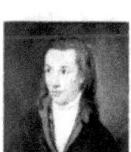
Joseph Conrad: *Heart of Darkness*
In the Dim Void: Samuel Beckett
Samuel Beckett Goes into the Silence
André Gide: Fiction and Fervour
Jackie Collins and the Blockbuster Novel
Blinded By Her Light: The Love-Poetry of Robert Graves
The Passion of Colours: Travels In Mediterranean Lands
Poetic Forms

POETRY

Ursula Le Guin: Walking In Cornwall
Peter Redgrove: Here Comes The Flood
Peter Redgrove: Sex-Magic-Poetry-Cornwall
Dante: Selections From the Vita Nuova
Petrarch, Dante and the Troubadours
William Shakespeare: Sonnets
William Shakespeare: Complete Poems
Blinded By Her Light: The Love-Poetry of Robert Graves
Emily Dickinson: Selected Poems
Emily Brontë: Poems
Thomas Hardy: Selected Poems
Percy Bysshe Shelley: Poems
John Keats: Selected Poems
Joh n Keats: Poems of 1820
D.H. Lawrence: Selected Poems
Edmund Spenser: Poems
Edmund Spenser: Amoretti
John Donne: Poems
Henry Vaughan: Poems
Sir Thomas Wyatt: Poems
Robert Herrick: Selected Poems
Rilke: Space, Essence and Angels in the Poetry of Rainer Maria Rilke
Rainer Maria Rilke: Selected Poems
Friedrich Hölderlin: Selected Poems
Arseny Tarkovsky: Selected Poems
Arthur Rimbaud: Selected Poems
Arthur Rimbaud: A Season in Hell
Arthur Rimbaud and the Magic of Poetry
Novalis: Hymns To the Night
German Romantic Poetry
Paul Verlaine: Selected Poems
Elizaethan Sonnet Cycles
D.J. Enright: By-Blows
Jeremy Reed: Brigitte's Blue Heart
Jeremy Reed: Claudia Schiffer's Red Shoes
Gorgeous Little Orpheus
Radiance: New Poems
Crescent Moon Book of Nature Poetry
Crescent Moon Book of Love Poetry
Crescent Moon Book of Mystical Poetry
Crescent Moon Book of Elizabethan Love Poetry
Crescent Moon Book of Metaphysical Poetry
Crescent Moon Book of Romantic Poetry
Pagan America: New American Poetry

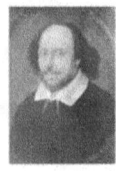
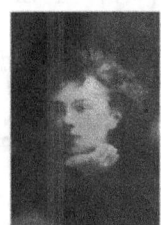
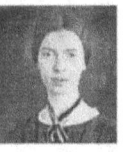
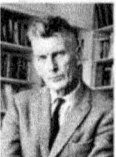
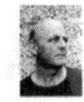
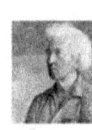
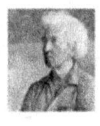
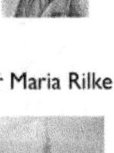
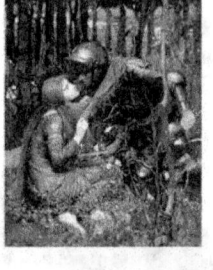
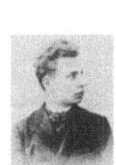
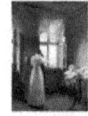

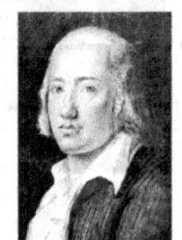

MEDIA, CINEMA, FEMINISM and CULTURAL STUDIES

J.R.R. Tolkien: The Books, The Films, The Whole Cultural Phenomenon
J.R.R. Tolkien: Pocket Guide
The *Lord of the Rings* Movies: Pocket Guide
The Cinema of Hayao Miyazaki
Hayao Miyazaki: *Princess Mononoke*: Pocket Movie Guide
Hayao Miyazaki: *Spirited Away*: Pocket Movie Guide
Tim Burton : Hallowe'en For Hollywood
Ken Russell
Ken Russell: *Tommy*: Pocket Movie Guide
The Ghost Dance: The Origins of Religion
The Peyote Cult
Cixous, Irigaray, Kristeva: The *Jouissance* of French Feminism
Julia Kristeva: Art, Love, Melancholy, Philosophy, Semiotics and Psychoanalysis
Luce Irigaray: Lips, Kissing, and the Politics of Sexual Difference
Hélene Cixous I Love You: The *Jouissance* of Writing
Andrea Dworkin
'Cosmo Woman': The World of Women's Magazines
Women in Pop Music
HomeGround: The Kate Bush Anthology
Discovering the Goddess (Geoffrey Ashe)
The Poetry of Cinema
The Sacred Cinema of Andrei Tarkovsky
Andrei Tarkovsky: Pocket Guide
Andrei Tarkovsky: *Mirror*: Pocket Movie Guide
Andrei Tarkovsky: *The Sacrifice*: Pocket Movie Guide
Walerian Borowczyk: Cinema of Erotic Dreams
Jean-Luc Godard: The Passion of Cinema
Jean-Luc Godard: *Hail Mary*: Pocket Movie Guide
Jean-Luc Godard: *Contempt*: Pocket Movie Guide
Jean-Luc Godard: *Pierrot le Fou*: Pocket Movie Guide
John Hughes and Eighties Cinema
Ferris Bueller's Day Off: Pocket Movie Guide
Jean-Luc Godard: Pocket Guide
The Cinema of Richard Linklater
Liv Tyler: Star In Ascendance
Blade Runner and the Films of Philip K. Dick
Paul Bowles and Bernardo Bertolucci
Media Hell: Radio, TV and the Press
An Open Letter to the BBC
Detonation Britain: Nuclear War in the UK
Feminism and Shakespeare
Wild Zones: Pornography, Art and Feminism
Sex in Art: Pornography and Pleasure in Painting and Sculpture
Sexing Hardy: Thomas Hardy and Feminism

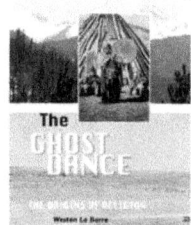
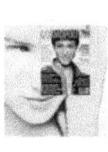
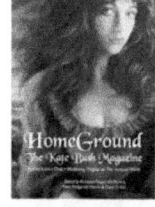

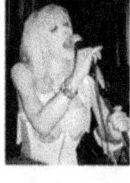
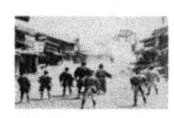
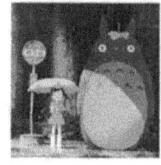
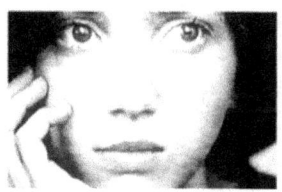

The Light Eternal is a model monograph, an exemplary job. The subject matter of the book is beautifully
organised and dead on beam. (Lawrence Durrell)
It is amazing for me to see my work treated with such passion and respect. (Andrea Dworkin)

CRESCENT MOON PUBLISHING
P.O. Box 1312, Maidstone, Kent, ME14 5XU, Great Britain. www.crmoon.com

cresmopub@yahoo.co.uk   www.crescentmoon.org.uk

www.ingramcontent.com/pod-product-compliance
Lightning Source LLC
Chambersburg PA
CBHW071323220526
45468CB00001B/476